M000318297

LOOK BOTH WAYS

ILLUSTRATED ESSAYS ON THE INTERSECTION OF LIFE AND DESIGN

WRITTEN AND ILLUSTRATED BY DEBBIE MILLMAN

DESIGNED BY RODRIGO CORRAL

HOW
BOOKS

CINCINNATI, OHIO
WWW.HOWDESIGN.COM

For more excellent books and resources for designers, visit www.howdesign.com.

13 12 11 10 09   5 4 3 2 1

Distributed in Canada by Fraser Direct
100 Armstrong Avenue
Georgetown, Ontario, Canada L7G 5S4
Tel: (905) 877-4411

Distributed in the U.K. and Europe by David & Charles
Brunel House, Newton Abbot, Devon, TQ12 4PU, England
Tel: (+44) 1626-323200, Fax: (+44) 1626-323319
E-mail: postmaster@davidandcharles.co.uk

Distributed in Australia by Capricorn Link
P.O. Box 704, Windsor, NSW 2756 Australia
Tel: (02) 4577-3555

Library of Congress Cataloging-in-Publication Data

Millman, Debbie.
  Look both ways / Debbie Millman. -- 1st ed.
    p. cm.
  ISBN 978-1-60061-321-0 (hardcover with jacket : alk. paper)
  1. Design--Psychological aspects. I. Title.
  NK1520.M56 2009
  745.401--dc22   2009022293

Editor: Jeremy Lehrer
Designer: Rodrigo Corral

HOW Books Managing Editor: Amy Schell
HOW Books Art Director: Grace Ring
Production Coordinator: Greg Nock

Excerpts of the following works appear in this book by permission of the copyright holders or by standards of fair use:

The Infinite Book: A Short Guide to the Timeless, Boundless and Endless, by John D. Barrow, published by Random House, Inc.

The Internet Encyclopedia of Science. Excerpts appear courtesy of David Darling.

"Let It Be," by John Lennon and Paul McCartney. Copyright 1970 Sony/ATV Tunes LLC. All rights administered by Sony/ATV Music Publishing, 8 Music Square West, Nashville, TN 37203. All rights reserved. Used by permission.

Letter from Robert Frost to Louis Untermeyer. Excerpted with the permission of the Estate of Robert Lee Frost.

Remembrance of Things Past: Volume 1, by Marcel Proust, translated by C.K. Scott Moncrieff and Terence Kilmartin, published by Random House, Inc.

Safe: Design Takes on Risk, edited and with introduction by Paola Antonelli, copyright © 2005 The Museum of Modern Art, New York.

"Same Old Song, but With a Different Meaning" by Shankar Vedantam. From *The Washington Post,* January 22, 2007 © 2007 *The Washington Post.* All rights reserved. Used by permission and protected by the Copyright Laws of the United States. The printing, copying, redistribution, or retransmission of the Material without express written permission is prohibited.

"Zweck or the Aim" by Ezra Pound, from *GUIDE TO KULCHUR,* copyright ©1970 by Ezra Pound. Reprinted by permission of New Directions Publishing Corp.

*To Sandra Kiersky, for helping
me understand my past*

*To Edwin Rivera, for helping
me understand my future*

CONTENTS

1   **HER STORY IS STRANGE**

7   **YELLOW**

17   **MY FIRST LOVE**

23   **THE LETTER H**

27   **FUDGETOWN**

37   **DOT FOR SHORT**

49   **DEBUTANTE**

63   **HELLO, DOLLY!**

73   **LEVI'S AND LACOSTE**

83   **CHEESE**

101   **LET IT BE**

113   **IF THAT HADN'T HAPPENED**

125   **PICK ONE**

137   **ECONOMY FOAM**

147   **NECESSARY OBJECTS**

161   **PEONIES**

171   **LOST IN TRANSLATIONS**

179   **FINAL FRONTIER**

191   **FAIL SAFE**

199   **LOOK BOTH WAYS**

HER STORY IS STRANGE

A few years ago, I attended Maira Kalman and Nico Muhly's opera "The Elements of Style," which was based on the landmark guide to grammatical usage written by William Strunk Jr. and E.B. White. The performance coincided with the release of Maira's illustrated version of the book. The opera was presented for one night only at the New York Public Library, and the show was entirely sold out.

In an effort to manage the large crowd, ushers holding way-finding signs were situated all along the line snaking through the library. Interspersed among the directional posters were whimsical placards handmade by Maira, featuring quirky and fanciful lines from the book. This pre-show exhibit was en-chanting. But my heart stopped when I noticed a woman holding a sign that simply stated what I considered to be the most mesmerizing line of all. The phrase, handwritten in Maira's sweet unmistakable script, read as follows:

"HER STORY
is STRANGE."

I couldn't help what I did next. I ran up to the young girl and asked if I could have the sign. She replied no, she needed it until the show began. I then asked if I could have it after the opera was over and offered to give her all the money I had in my wallet. She looked embarrassed and suggested that I try to find her after the performance. In the meantime, she would ask the people in charge if she was allowed to give the piece away.

After what could be described as a truly magnificent opera, the audience gathered for a post-show reception. I scanned the room, searching for the young usher, and when I finally found her, I inquired again about the object of my desire. She responded that she had forgotten to ask her boss and told me she would try to find her.

An eternity passed, and finally she returned and explained that before giving away the piece, her boss needed to ask Maira's permission to part with it. Maira had a question for the person who wanted the cardboard sign. Since the placard read "HER STORY IS STRANGE," Maira wanted to know if indeed my story was strange. I looked this affable young woman right in the eye and, without missing a beat, I gleefully and proudly stated that YES!, most assuredly, my story was strange. And with that, my new friend smiled wide, pulled the prized artwork from behind her back, and replied, "Then yes. If your story is strange, then yes," Maira said you can have it."

STRANGe

YELLOW

When I was a little girl, visiting my father's pharmacy was one of my favorite pastimes. I was dazzled by all of the branded wares that neatly lined the mahogany shelves, and I would spend hours ogling the packaging.

As I examined the illustrations, designs and photographs, my imagination took over: I invented stories about the babies on the Gerber products; I'd pretend to apply the CoverGirl makeup; I'd endlessly analyze the girl on the beach shown on the Stayfree sanitary napkin packaging.

The crown jewel in my father's store was the barrette display. This ~~way~~ was a shrine of

Sparkling magical wonder—a spinning cascade of glamour, hope, and desire. And while I saw lots of other brands of barrettes in numerous stores, my father carried only the Goody brand. The Goody showcase display held every possible hair accessory: head bands, bobby pins, colorful plastic clips in the shape of butterflies, bows in velvet and gingham, a myriad of hair brushes, combs, shower caps, and my favorite hair accoutrement of all—ponytail holders, sold in packages of four, eight or an eyepopping 20.

The ponytail holders were constructed of two round baubles held together by an elastic band. The packs were organized by size (small, medium, and large) and by style—with some translucent and others opaque; each set contained beads in an assortment of primary and secondary colors. At the end of each sojourn at the store, my father allowed me to choose one package to take home.

As I contemplated my selection, I would stand in front of the display for what seemed like an eternity, slowly spinning it round and round, overwhelmed by the magnitude of my choice: What should I take? Which was the most beautiful? What would make me look the prettiest? After

I made my decision, I would bring home my coveted treasure, carefully open the pack, spread out my newly obtained amulets, and then... I would do nothing. I wouldn't do my hair up, and I didn't try on the ponytail holders. I just stared at them in divine intoxication. I was content to look at them and add them to my lovely, expanding trove. I felt rich with accomplishment and dizzy with glee. No one had the collection that I had; no one could be as lucky as I was.

My best friend at the time, a very petite blonde-haired girl named Andrea, lived next door. We did everything together, and we were very much kindred spirits. We shared our deepest secrets, and we would spend hours and hours planning our futures. We dreamed about who we would be, where we would travel, and what we would wear. While we had a close camaraderie, Andrea did not share my penchant for hair accessories. She tolerated my burgeoning collection, but she had no desire to join me in my trinket worship.

One day when we were playing at her house, I noticed a small ponytail holder on her bureau, and I was immediately mesmerized and perplexed. I had never seen a specimen of that style or that hue—a pearly pale yellow—ever. Of course, it was made by Goody. Whenever I went over to Andrea's house during subsequent weeks, I always looked for the barrette, and it was always there, in the same place. Every time I went to my father's drugstore, I looked to see if he had that pale yellow variety, and he never did. Suddenly I was angry and jealous. I wanted that ponytail holder— and Andrea was the only one who had it.

For better or worse, this little object—this little brand—transformed me. Brands can do that. They're capable of creating intimate worlds that only their inhabitants can understand, worlds where each citizen has a meaningful identity and a sense of belonging. Brands create tribes. They allow us to assert moods, tastes, whims, and choice. Brands signal our affiliations and can even define our beliefs. In a time when our culture is so diverse, brands enable us to simultaneously stand out and fit in. For whatever sad reason, my childhood barrettes buoyed up an otherwise fragile ego. They provided me with a social confidence I may not have otherwise had, however illusory its foundation. These silly little hair accessories gave me something to have pride in, when I didn't have pride in myself.

My fervent obsession with these objects led me to continue fixating on Andrea's yellow pony-tail holder. I was angry and jealous. I wanted the barrette, and I didn't know how to get it.

One afternoon, unable to stop myself, when my best friend wasn't looking, I took the treasure off her bureau and put it in my pocket. I stole Andrea's yellow ponytail holder.

For weeks after the crime, I waited for Andrea to notice, but she never did. But for me, our friendship was irrevocably changed. Andrea and I used to talk about everything, and now I had a terrible secret we couldn't share. I couldn't face her anymore, and we drifted apart. I began to hate myself because of my desire and my greed. Brands can be many things; those who support brands and those who decry them, such as the no logo crowd, have passionate views on the subject. What I can tell you about brands is this: Maybe they can make you feel more beautiful, or sexier, or cooler, or more hip or alluring. What they do not ~~can~~ have the power to do is make you a better person. Brands can't do that. There is no sneaker in the world, no burger chain, no cocktail, no barrette that can make you a kinder, more interesting, more loveable person. Only we can do that for ourselves.

MY FIRST LOVE

I am and will always be deeply sentimental. I still own many of the books from my childhood, the first sports medal I won in fourth grade (for a three-legged race), an old Band-Aid tin, and the business card on which an old boyfriend scribbled his phone number when we first met. | That same man often accused me of an excessive degree of hero worship. I attributed this trait to my sentimentality, which gives me an irrepressible desire to collect and admire images, artifacts and memorabilia from the defining moments in my life; to gather mementos of ideas and experiences that provoke and move me; and to assemble around me things I want close by as amulets of inspiration. My paramour was at first perplexed but then put off by my curious fascination with popular culture and its hierarchies of fame and power. | I have been analyzing this oft-criticized, seamy

worship of mine though the years, seeking to understand its origin in my psyche. I remember anxiously awaiting my
favorite Friday night television shows as my
infatuations flitted from David Cassidy in The Partridge
Family to Lee Majors in The Six Million Dollar
Man. Digging deeper into my emotional history, I remember
kissing the television when Mr. Rogers came
on. I remember being obsessed with Marcia Brady, Olivia Newton-John, New York Rangers Hall of Famer
Eddie Giacomin, and the NHL mascot Peter Puck. | But I didn't
know and couldn't seem to discover why I needed
and constructed this worship. What did I admire most? What
was I trying to gain? While I recognized what
these performers, artists and entertainers might stand for—or
might bring to me through my experience of
them—I realized that it was what I was bringing to the idea of
them that was important to comprehend. I
realized that I was bestowing all sorts of magical and unreal-
istic fantasies and expectations on these figures.
I am still not sure why—it seems that as a culture we are
held captive by the comparisons we make be-
tween ourselves and others; many of the people we admire or
despise, similar to the brands we collect or cringe
at, not only signify our beliefs but have come to define them. |
Still not satisfied with the results of my
internal investigation, I put the whole exercise on hold, content
with the knowledge that this silly, sentimental
adulation—this objectification of fantasy and perfection

that brought me to believe an object could bestow "happiness always"—was neither realistic nor honorable; the origin of this cult of personality continued to seem out of reach. | Until last winter. Miserably saddled with a cold that knocked me out, I decided, as I planned my exit strategy from the world, to go to the market and purchase the ingredients for my grandmother's chicken soup. I would cook up a big pot, and I could live on it for days, if need be. I stumbled into my local Gristede's and thoughtlessly tossed all the necessary soup accoutrements—crisp, leafy parsley, bumpy turnips, pearl barley—into my cart. Then I had what seemed to be an epiphany (please note: I was running a fever)—I would treat myself to a bubble bath! | Sniffling and out of breath, I bounded over to the personal products aisle. And then in one powerful, provocative (and nearly painful) Proustian moment, it all came back to me. My first love. My earliest taste of sentimental objectification. My original encounter with hero worship. My initial freefall into the phenomenal world of imagination and fantasy. I saw him again as I saw him for the first time—the one who started it all: Mr. Bubble. | When I was a child, Mr. Bubble granted me "happiness always." Before my daily encounter with him, I felt unseemly, and afterwards I was bright and shiny. Bath time before bedtime allowed me to slide into rosy, joyful dreamland. The experience of Mr. Bubble always matched exactly what I had anticipated. Mr. Bubble was funny and cute. He made me laugh. Way before Mr. Rogers, before Barbie, Levi's and Lacoste, Mr. Bubble was my first love, my first celebrity. My first brand. | My rendezvous with Mr. Bubble led me to reflect more deeply on why brand icons from the past were so compelling. Decades before we were entertained and titillated by Madonna and Cher, womenfolk like Rosie and Betty delighted us. We all know Madonna and Cher; like many of their superstar peers, they are celebrities, entertainers, and—most of all—brands who emerged during the second half of the 20th century. But Rosie and Betty were first-class celebrities of the first half. The characters Rosie the Riveter and Betty Crocker were created by artists and graphic designers to entertain us, distract us, sell products, or give us purpose, and to also make us feel better about the world and who we are. | This was emotional branding in its infancy. After these characters were invented, people began to wonder what the Morton Salt girl was "really" like. Men even called General Mills to propose to Betty Crocker. McCall's Magazine created a Betsy McCall paper doll for the pages of the magazine and introduced a three-dimensional doll into toy stores. | Sadly, this type of graphic art seems to be disappearing in favor of fluorescent celebrities and mega-branded lifestyles. Or maybe the ability of these characters to hold sway over our imaginations has faded in these reality show, Us Weekly days. No longer do we imagine what Betty

Crocker might be like "in real life." But I hold out hope for what I believe is timeless—a desire to be surrounded by the people, pets and artifacts that we love, and the endearing characters that give us permission to play and imagine. And I can rest assured, knowing that no matter how complicated life becomes, there is always a box of Mr. Bubble waiting for me at home.

THE LETTER H

From the time I was very little, I loved to make things. I made my own coloring books, paper dolls, and dioramas, and I even tried to make my own perfume by crushing rose petals into baby oil. I made barrette boxes out of Popsicle sticks, key chains out of lanyards, ashtrays out of clay, and Halloween costumes out of construction paper and old bedsheets. I grew up in a household with a strong do-it-yourself mentality and a mom who made a living as a painter and a seamstress, so I received numerous accolades for my artistic inclinations. I also found that making things by hand gave me a strong sense of accomplishment and pride. When I started kindergarten, I faced the first obstacle to my theretofore unmitigated creative prowess. As I was first learning to write, it became clear that I had trouble creating certain letterforms. I had a particular difficulty placing the little tail on the capital *Q*; I had problems discerning the lowercase *d* from the lowercase *b* (which was of significant concern, given my first name). I also discovered I had artistic and intellectual blockages relating to the capital *H*. For some reason, I had trouble constructing two parallel lines connected in the center by a horizontal one. I couldn't draw any of the lines straight, and I couldn't seem to create a consistent spacing between the vertical lines. I was unable to get an even weight for all three strokes. My mother became so exasperated with me that she enlisted my grandmother to take over the fraught endeavor. As I continued to struggle, and as my anguish turned to wrath, I reached an impasse I had never encountered before: I couldn't do something I'd set out to do. While one might surmise that the inability of a child to construct the letter *H* couldn't possibly have long-term ramifications, I confess that there were further complications I have not yet mentioned. All those years ago, I was not called Debbie. I was called Deborah, spelled *D-E-B-O-R-A-H*. Therefore, my ineptitude in drawing an *H* was rather worrisome. As my mighty efforts grew futile and my temper tantrum intensified over the many mangled letterforms, my grandmother cleverly came to a realization: Since I had recently mastered my *d*'s and *b*'s, I would be able to spell "Debbie"! The name Deborah would no longer be an obstacle to my self-expression. And thus, a new moniker emerged, one that has lasted ever since. And it was in that initial transformation that I first fell in love with the agile, malleable, and thoroughly magical acrobatics of lettering, language, and communication. This *aventure d'amour* has continued throughout my life. And I still have a preference for doing almost everything by hand. In a day and age when nanotechnology and computer science have ushered in an era of seamless digitalia, I believe there is a profound beauty in all things handmade. While computers might set type in flawlessly accurate columns, handcrafted artwork and design are beautiful by virtue of their irregularity. I see these imperfections as marks of dignity and integrity, and believe that they bear witness to the artist—and the human—in all of us. Now all grown up, I have a fascination with any handmade object containing the written word. I find myself transfixed by the confluence of art and design evident in the "typographic" missives of Ed Fella, Lawrence Weiner, and Paula Scher, not to mention the heartbreakingly poignant narration handwritten in the work of Cy Twombly and Philip Guston. What I find resonant in these objects is an inherent authenticity and honesty. These creations preserve an enduring, uniquely human imprint. As we deconstruct our lives in the search for meaning, it is these handcrafted messages that have the magnitude—and the soul—to measure, reflect, and express who we are. I recently came across one of the most ambitious projects I ever undertook as a young adult: a completely handwritten, hand-drawn magazine that I created in collaboration with my best friend at the time, also named Debbie. In honor of our efforts and our teenage aspirations, we named it *Debutante*. We made sure the title didn't contain an *H*.

FUDGETOWN

My favorite cookie of all time, the
Fudgetown, was made by Keebler. Fudgetowns
were chocolate sandwich cookies popular when
I was a young girl, and I thought they were
the most delectable and beautiful cookies
ever created. They were delectable because
the milk chocolate in them was soft and
fudgy, and because the sandwich biscuits
were crispy and flaky, with an O-shaped hole
in the middle of them leading to the lus-
cious cocoa cream interior. They were beautiful because they were shaped liked flowers, with a thick dollop of chocolate on the
inside pushing out through the sides as well
as the top and bottom of the biscuits.

I used to savor the experience of these cookies slowly: First, I would stick my tongue into the middle to flick out the chocolaty dollop from the biscuit center, then I would pop open the two sandwich pieces and use my teeth to scrape off the remaining chocolate on the inside. Afterwards, I would keep each cookie on my tongue until it melted away in my mouth. This ritual probably took about 20 minutes, but the memory of the experience has lasted a lifetime. And while I also cherished my moments with Wise Bar-B-Q Potato Chips, Drake's Yodels, Cheez Doodles, and Grape Nehi soda, the Fudgetown cookies alone still make my knees tremor with love and devotion.

As if the heavenly taste of the cookies themselves wasn't enough, I also fell under the spell of the package containing these blissful morsels. The wrappings featured the Keebler Elves, of course, but inasmuch as I found these brand icons amusing and enter-taining, it was not the Elves that captured my interest. What utterly mesmerized me was the illustration on the front panel of the cookie package, which showed the Keebler Elves holding a package of Fudgetown cookies. This meant that the Keebler Elves were holding a package of Fudgetown cookies featuring the Keebler Elves holding a package of Fudgetown cookies. And so on and so on and so on. The Keebler Elves holding the package showing the Keebler Elves holding the package was an infinitely recurring series. This killed me!

I would stare at the package for hours on end, trying to pinpoint the moment I could see the singularity: where the Keebler Elves and the cookie package both originated. It all ended up in a single point that was indiscernible, and I was both entranced and perplexed by the notion of this infinite repetition. This became my entrée to the concept of infinity, and I found the philosophic conundrum it represented and the unresolved mystery of it to be wondrous and stupefying.

Infinity is "a concept that has always fascinated philosophers and theologians, linked as it is to the notions of unending distance or space, eternity, and God," explains scientist David Darling in his online Encyclopedia of Science. While some thinkers eagerly entertained thoughts of infinity, Darling notes that in mathematics the idea was met with derision. "Only within the past century or so," he observes, "have mathematicians dealt with it head on and accepted infinity as a number—albeit the strangest one we know."

As author John Barrow writes in The Infinite Book, "Infinity remains a fascinating subject. It lies at the heart of all sorts of fundamental human questions. Can you live forever? Will the Universe have an end? Did it have a beginning? Does the Universe have an 'edge' or is it simply unbounded in size? Although it is easy to think about lists of numbers or sequences of clock ticks that go on forever, there are other sorts of infinity that seem to be more challenging. What about an infinite temperature or an infinite brightness? Can such physical things actually be infinite? Or is infinity just shorthand for 'finite but awfully big'?"

My search for the origin point on the Fudgetown cookie box led to other dalliances with the illusory magic of packaging. The obsession came to include Goody brand barrette packaging, Golden Books covers, all things Barbie (of course), as well as record covers of albums by Olivia Newton-John, Elton John, and the band Yes—when the group's albums were illustrated by Roger Dean. Band-Aid tins, the Morton Salt girl, and McCall's Magazine's Betsy McCall also figured prominently in my fascination with consumer icons. This conglomeration of items, ideas, designs, culture, and iconographies fits into what I now romantically and proudly call "branding."

The upside to all of this brand attachment is just that: feeling connected, part of something larger than oneself, and participating in a real or imagined community of like-minded spirits. The downside, of course, is multifaceted. First: These communities may very well have a shaky foundation. After all, it's hard to depend on the reliability and support system of transitional objects, which most of these icons and products usually are.

Second: There comes a point when you realize that these things, these brands, aren't "enough." Having more or better or best doesn't provide you with a lasting sense of having more or being better or being best. It's a rather fleeting experience, this romantic attachment to brands, and I find that if I'm not careful, the search for having more or better or best is a precarious journey into the infinite. When you depend on finite objects—or brands—to provide you with a long-term sense of self or love or pride or achievement, you start yourself out on a path with no end. No object, no product, and no brand can provide you with ultimate, infinite satisfaction.

I once had a boyfriend tell me I was a bottomless pit of need. He wasn't saying this because I thought I needed another pair of shoes or a Prada handbag (which I likely did at the time, but that's another story entirely), but rather because of a fragile emotional state that led me to crave constant reassurances of my lovability. As you can imagine, this drove him crazy. My infinite need for reassurance required an infinite effort on his part, and you can guess how that relationship turned out.

Some infinities are tough. Others, like the concept of infinite space or other mathematical abstractions, are simply inconceivable. But I believe some infinities are worthy challenges: the search for what is truly beautiful; laughing at the same time with someone you love; discovering a perfect piece of poetry; experiencing the deepest feelings of empathy. If that doesn't work, there are always chocolate cookies, but I do think T.S. Eliot describes it best in his poem "Preludes":

His soul stretched tight across the skies
That fade behind a city block,
Or trampled by insistent feet
At four and five and six o'clock
And short square fingers stuffing pipes,
And evening newspapers, and eyes
Assured of certain certainties,
The conscience of a blackened street
Impatient to assume the world.

I am moved by fancies that are curled
Around these images, and cling:
The notion of some infinitely gentle
Infinitely suffering thing.

Wipe your hand across your mouth, and laugh;
The worlds revolve like ancient women
Gathering fuel in vacant lots.

DOT FOR SHORT

When I was a kid, there were lots of rules in my house. One of the most horrific concerned the very limited amount of television I was allowed to watch. As a result of the boob tube embargo, I read. And I read a lot. I read books, magazines, newspapers, encyclopedias and comic books; I even borrowed my mother's REDBOOK and McCALLS and SNUCK into my father's library to read the steamy sections of THE GODFATHER when I was sure that no one would catch me. My fascination with books began as SOON AS I could read, and Golden Books were my favorites. Then came my introduction to the WEEKLY READER- the classroom magazine for elementary and pre-K students -there was nothing, Absolutely nothing, I looked forward to more than the moment, every week, when our teacher, Mrs. Mayer handed out those glamorous publications, filled with all sorts of, useful information, games, and facts. By third grade, I became acquainted with The Scholastic BOOK CLUB, and while my folks were stingy with television privileges, they were quite generous with my book allowance. I ordered as many books as I could afford, and when the boxes came in with my name on them, I spent a MOMENT gingerly fingering the corrugated brown carton. I'd sit for a minute or two and imagine what was inside, anticipating what the books could conjure, and, of course, how they would look. The universe I entered when I read these books was in part visual. I studied the illustrations and paintings of my precious tomes as intently as I read the words yearning to teletransport into these two-dimensional galaxies in order to make them my own. After the Scholastic phase came the series books: Nancy Drew, Trixie Belden, and my all-time beloved: the stories of Ginnie and Geneva by Catherine Woolley. These series became mirrors into a different universe. A place where, despite danger or mishaps or misdeeds, life was always good, the bad guys were always caught and everyone always lived happily ever after. These worlds were foreign to me, and I constantly projected myself into those books: I became the characters and lived their challenges — and grew so much richer for the experience.

I don't know what happened to all my books. My family moved around a lot when I was growing up, and since most of the books were paperbacks, I guess my parents didn't ferry them from house to house. So for the last several decades, I have been scouring, used book-stores, libraries, garage sales, and flea markets for all the BOOKS I read as a child. I am extremely particular about what I purchase: the Golden Books must

42

have the gorgeous GOLD-and-brown metallic trim intact; the Nancy DREW editions must have the hardcover yellow spine and the illustrations in the cover plate. I will only buy Ginnie books featuring

illustrations by Liz Dauber
OR Iris Beatty Johnson,
and I limit myself to
vintage Trixies with Larry
Frederick's cover illustrations.
I have been extraordinarily lucky
in tracking down many of these classics;
nevertheless several titles
have proved more elusive.

One was a book
called DOT FOR SHORT, by Frieda
Friedman. This was a charming,
bittersweet story written in 1947
about an insecure girl,
Dot, who can't wait to grow up.
As Friedman writes "She envies
her two gorgeous sisters (Fluff
and Peg) who are tall and slender
and know how to talk to boys."

HER family is having financial difficulties, which Dot feels helpless to improve. Then she sees an ad in a ladies' magazine featuring a contest to write a limerick about "why you use Masterpiece Muffin Mix." The prize is $10,000. Dot, of course, writes a limerick, and... well, that's all I am going to tell you. Needless to say, at the time I read it, the 'entire scenario of the book narrative converged with my own life and even my fledging enchantment with— dare I say it— branding. In light of all that, Dot For Short is very dear to me. All through the '80's, I not only searched through flea markets and the like for this pesky novel, I also went into every mass-market and private bookseller to inquire about it. Numerous storekeepers were sympathetic to my quest and often suggested I order the title— optimistically suggesting that a used bookstore might come across it if we initiated a nationwide search. I did that over and over, but to no avail. Then, one day in 1988, as I was conducting my usual perusal in the children's section of a bookstore, there it was. Reprinted. Fresh and clean and new and... mine. I grabbed it, gave my money to the cashier with shaking hands and read the entire book out on the street, leaning against a light pole. It was a magical, unforgettable experience.

46

My Library is now nearly complete.

Every now and then, I remember a book that I read when I was eight or eleven or sixteen... the memory flutters into my head like a yellow butterfly and then I am inspired to once again start a new search. I love this recreation of sorts; knowing that I am simultaneously rebuilding and recrafting my present and my future.

Knowing, as Proust observed of Swann's moment with a madeleine, that these books "ultimately reach the clear surface of my consciousness, this memory, this old, dead moment which the magnetism of an identical moment has traveled so far to importune, to disturb, to raise up out of the depths of my being... and bear unfaltering, in the tiny and almost impalpable drop of their essence, the vast structure of recollection."

DEBUTANTE

When I was 12 years old, my best friend was also named Debbie. She, like me, loved magazines and fashion, and we both loved to write, draw, and paint. The summer before we went into sixth grade, we spent the entire break creating a magazine, which—because we were both named Debbie—we titled Debutante. We spent endless hours writing all the articles in longhand and illustrating numerous pictures. We became consumed with the creation of this publication.

We interviewed people we
knew for "tell-all" articles and
we initiated our own surveys
about boys, clothes, and
even kissing—though I doubt
either of us by that age had
ever kissed anyone, at least
not romantically. We went
through all of our existing
magazines and books for
ideas, and we were deliriously
and passionately obsessed
with our creation. We loved
making all our own decisions
about what to include and
what to exclude, and what
we deemed culturally
important—and not—in that
summer of 1973. The only
argument we had during that

time concerned who was
going to keep the original
copy. It was one of the
most perfect summers I
ever had.

For me, DIY was not a novel
concept. My mother, a
single-parent divorcee,
supported our family as a
seamstress. Because we
didn't have much money, the
first recourse for anything
we wanted or needed was to
make it ourselves. My school
lunches were bagged, my
school textbook covers were
designed by my mom, and
though I was profoundly
embarrassed about it at the

time, most of my clothes
were handmade—sewn either
by Mom, by me, or knitted
by my grandmother.

My homemade wardrobe
included embroidered red
corduroy overalls complete
with a matching bolero
jacket, a hot pink puffy-
sleeved shirt with a purple
butterfly appliqued on the
front, and a sky blue cable-
knit fisherman's sweater
with a matching hat. I
actually made a skirt to
match the pink puffy shirt,
but when ironing the rather
complicated pleated front, I
scorched the skirt. You can

only imagine how I felt—there
was no consoling me that
day.

All through junior high school,
I looked longingly at the
other girls in their cool Levi's
jeans and their lovely (and
professionally made) designer
shirts. I envied the clothes'
store-bought crispness and
the girls' effortless fashion
sophistication. I felt shabby
and meager in comparison.

Back then, there seemed to
be a profound difference
between doing something
myself when I wanted to,
and doing something myself

when I had no other choice.
Making my own magazine
was a thrill and a challenge;
making my own wardrobe—or
having my mother make it
for me—felt like a humiliation.

Until last Christmas. Every
year, as the months wind
down and the holidays begin,
I take two weeks off from
work and try to complete 12
months' worth of errands
and "home improvements."
The days are jam-packed
with necessary chores like
having the chimney swept,
silly but deeply fulfilling
projects like alphabetizing my
CDs, or perpetually lingering

tasks like finally cleaning out the closet underneath the stairs. This year, I actually got to the pesky and pernicious closet stuffed with boxes of books, abandoned knick-knacks, badly rewired lamps, broken speakers, paint cans, and power tools.

I took everything out and opened up every box and bag. There were cartons I hadn't opened in 20 years—they had remained taped shut from move to move, as I remained reluctant to throw out anything I might one day miss. As I perused through photo albums, wedding albums, college textbooks, journals, letters, and postcards, I relived three decades of my life on waves of laughter, tears, snickers, shrieks, and groans. After two days, I was down to two boxes. I was ready to give up the task, as I was both physically and emotionally exhausted.

Nevertheless, I pressed on. And when I opened the boxes, I discovered neat piles of clothes: sweaters and jackets, hats and blouses. These were the outfits that my mother and grandmother had made for me. There was the blouse, complete with neck bow, that I wore to a job interview in the early '80s; a brown tie-dyed cowboy jacket with a groovy polyester leopard-print lining; a navy blue bolero jacket with embroidered trim; and... the sky blue fisherman's sweater, with its matching hat.

My heart stopped when I took in the abundance of what I had uncovered. The sweater was the only sartorial memento that I had of my long-gone grand-mother, and the only evidence of her incredible handiwork. I held the clothes close to me and realized how much time, energy, and love must have gone into their creation. I became ashamed at how I was once embarrassed by the fact that they were handmade. And I realized then how much effort my mom and grandmother put into every detail as they strived to make me feel pretty, fashionable, and special.

We are living in a time now where knitting, sewing, and DIY crafts have become "au courant." One common

denominator in all of this
craft-making is that we are
doing what we love. In
reconsidering my own
family's efforts, I see that
our "doing it ourselves"
creations were really expres-
sions, and embodiments, of
love. When I think back to
Debutante, I recall how much
devotion my doppelganger
Debbie and I invested in the
magazine, and the bliss I
experienced in the process of
making it, and in its comple-
tion. And I realize now that
my mother and grandmother
must have found the same
delight when they devoted
so much care into making

clothes for me. These material items were sure signs of
their love, and held that
emotion—and still embody
it—in a way that no designer
creation ever could.

....

HELLO, DOLLY!

When I was eight years old, my mother sat me and my brother down in our living room and told us that she and my father were getting a divorce. She then proceeded to try and cheer us up by taking us to the movies, and she ferried us to see Barbra Streisand in the box-office hit Hello, Dolly! I remember my brother weeping as I watched Barbra convince Walter Matthau to eat his beets, telling him how good the beets were, that there was nothing quite as good as beets. To this day, I can't see a beet without thinking of divorce. Who knew that a red root vegetable could be so weighty with meaning?

I find it both curious and compelling that the moments of our lives are punctuated by visual images that, over time, become permanently embedded in the experience. There are few women I know who can't recall what they were wearing when they met the love of their life. Several men I know have powerful recollections of the Led Zeppelin album cover they were drifting into when they smoked pot for the first time. Other friends remember a particular clock in their grandparents' house, a singular sequence from an avant-garde film, or the look on a loved one's face when they found out someone close had died.

These visuals mark time for us, they represent age; they represent a moment when the narrative of the everyday is broken, because of love, or loss, or deep inspiration—experiences that shift the boundary of the possible.

I remember the grey corduroy suit I wore to the inaugural day of my first job in 1983. I remember the sparkly colors of a necklace that a cherished babysitter gave to me when I was six. I recall the bearing of an awkwardly bespectacled girl named Susan as she used the words "chimera" and "enigma" in an essay she read aloud in tenth-grade English; I remember the way a little girl in my kindergarten class drew grass in her many drawings, and how straight her bangs were. Individually, these are random images. Joined together, they reflect a life.

In pivotal moments of my personal history, fleeting metaphorical signs have made indelible impressions on me: The day I walked out of my apartment with an open heart and lofty hopes, I saw an open parking spot as a reassuring omen of the future. When I later saw a dead squirrel in the street, I was sure something horrible was about to happen. To celebrate my thirtieth birthday, I got all dressed up and went to the restaurant Elaine's with my husband and another couple. My favorite pearl necklace broke and the beads spilled out all over the floor around us. As everyone frantically ran to gather the mess of scattered pearls, I knew in that instant that my marriage was over.

The painter Mark Rothko alluded to these visual intuitions, and their power, as Bernard Malamud recalls in his heartbreaking introduction to the retrospective anthology Mark

Rothko: A Retrospective. Malamud writes: "Rothko liked to reminisce. One night he told me how he had left his first wife. He had gone off for an army physical during World War II and they had turned him down. When he arrived home and told his wife he was 4-F, he didn't like the look that flitted across her face. The next day he went to see his lawyer about a divorce."

These woeful images haunt me. Many years ago, I confronted a man who had hurt me badly when I was growing up. It literally took me years to get up the courage to face him, and, looking back on it now, I can't help but shake my head in amazement as I remember standing on the front porch of his house, shivering in the autumn chill. As I held myself tight in my yellow coat, the man's clueless wife kept calling out to her husband, insisting he invite me in for coffee and cake.

These visual mementos, visceral as they are, catalog our experiences. When I think about divorce, I ordinarily don't think about beets. But when I see beets, I inevitably think about divorce. We process our emotions, in part, through images. I'm certain this is why we are both drawn to and provoked by art in such powerful and profound ways, and ultimately why art is such a subjective and personal experience: It simultaneously allows us to feel emotions we might not otherwise be able to describe and evokes our own personal association with those very feelings.

I prefer to look back and remember the images, as opposed to what was actually said or accomplished or fucked up. I like to think that there is beauty and power in every one of these images. But as I hold them close, I also realize that they don't really exist. They are not anything I can touch. They are not archived in a photo album or hanging in a pretty frame. They are not neatly taped into a scrapbook, or downloaded and stored on Flickr or my iPod. But they live, and always will—in my imagination, and in my heart.

LEVI'S AND LACOSTE

My love affair with brands hit CRITICAL MASS when I was in the SEVENTH GRADE. I looked around and noticed everyone in school was wearing really cool pants with a little red tag on the back POCKET; the ubiquitous and CHIC fashion ensemble of the day included polo shirts featuring little crocodiles stitched into the fabric, above the heart. LEVI'S and LACOSTE:

The names that go along with these ICONOGRAPHIES are intimately familiar to us now. IN THOSE JUNIOR HIGH SCHOOL YEARS, Levi's and Lacoste clothes were expensive — as they still are — and my mother didn't understand why we had to pay more money for the RED TAG and the crocodile when the clothing without them was the same quality but cheaper. FURTHERMORE, because MOM was a seamstress, she didn't comprehend the appeal of buying something she could

make herself. SHE COMPROMISED
by offering to make THE VERY
SAME CLOTHES FROM SCRATCH.
She'd stitch a red tag into the
back pocket of the pants; she'd
glue a CROCODILE PATCH from the
Lee Wards craft store onto a perfectly
good polo shirt from MODELL'S.

While that plan didn't quite suit my asp-irations of being a seventh grade trend-setter — or of being voted the best-dressed girl at ELWOOD JUNIOR HIGH— I eagerly pored through the racks of Lee Wards, des-perately searching for a crocodile patch to stick onto the front of my favorite pink polo shirt. ALAS,

There was
nothing even
close.

The best substitute I came up with was a cute rendition of TONY THE TIGER, but that really wasn't the look or cachet I was going for.

I rode my bike home from Lee Wards DEJECTED AND MOPEY.

When my mom found out I hadn't been successful, I could see she felt sorry for me. So she took the matter into her own hands. The Lacoste —

shirts were too expensive,
but there were indeed some Levi's
on sale at the <u>WALT WHITMAN</u>
<u>MALL</u>, and she bought me a pair.
BUT she didn't get the denim
variety that everyone <u>else</u>
was wearing; she found a design
that must have been from the
triple-markdown racks— a pair
OF LIME GREEN
CORDUROY
BELL-BOTTOM

LEVI'S.

It was with a mixture of HORROR AND PRIDE that I paraded in front of the full-length mirror in my bedroom, ever so slightly sticking MY BUTT OUT so that I could be sure the little red tag would show. So what if I was wearing lime green corduroy! They were Levi's I was cool. The reign of logo worship had BEGUN.

CHEESE

WHEN I FIRST MOVED TO **MANHATTAN,**

I LIVED ON THE FOURTH FLOOR OF AN OLD TENEMENT BUILDING ON 16TH STREET.

I lived in a "**RAILROAD APARTMENT**" **WHERE YOU** HAD TO WALK THROUGH ONE ROOM to get to another.

MY BEDROOM WAS IN THE BACK OF THE BUILDING, AN ARRANGEMENT THAT WAS RATHER AWKWARD, ESPECIALLY SINCE

I SHARED THE APARTMENT WITH A SEXUALLY ACTIVE ON-AGAIN/OFF-AGAIN COUPLE.

I HAD TO WALK THROUGH THEIR BEDROOM IN ORDER TO GO INTO

OR OUT OF
MY ROOM,

and

I

never

knew

what

to

expect ON THE JOURNEY.

———

WE LIVED LIKE THIS UNTIL THEY BROKE UP,
AND BY THEN,
MERCIFULLY, I had enough money to pay the rent by myself.

THIS MEANT THAT I COULD WATCH WHATEVER

TELEVISION PROGRAM I WANTED TO, WHENEVER I WANTED TO,
AND I COULD LISTEN TO MY MUSIC—the Cocteau Twins,
This Mortal Coil, and Modern English—
AS LOUD AS I DAMN WELL PLEASED.

I ATTEMPTED TO DECORATE MY APARTMENT

IN A WAY THAT WAS MORE BEFITTING ADULTHOOD, **AND** AS SOON AS I SAVED ENOUGH MONEY,

I REPLACED THE DINGY MILK CRATES HOLDING MY BOOKS WITH A **REAL BOOKCASE** AND TRADED IN MY FLOOR-BOUND FUTON FOR A SLATTED BED WITH A HEADBOARD.

GIVEN MY PROFOUND LACK OF FUNDS, I FOUND MYSELF INVESTIGATING A **MYRIAD** OF DESIGN ALTERNATIVES

IN AN EFFORT TO CRAFT MY OWN VERSION OF **HOME SWEET HOME.**

I USED CONTACT PAPER TO WALLPAPER THE KITCHEN; I USED DOUBLE-SIDED TAPE TO STICK ON A FAUX TIN-TILE BACKSPLASH BEHIND THE SINK; and I CREATED CUSTOM FLOOR-TO-CEILING BOOKSHELVES WITH BRICKS FROM A LOCAL LUMBER STORE THAT I LUGGED UP THE FOUR FLIGHTS AND STACKED IN AN ALCOVE BY THE WINDOW.

I ALSO STARTED TO ENTERTAIN.
I BEGAN BY INVITING FAMILY AND FRIENDS, AND SLOWLY

EXPANDED THE GATHERINGS TO INCLUDE COLLEAGUES AND NEIGHBORS.

I ALSO EXPERIMENTED WITH COOKING

AND ENJOYED PRESENTING MY HANDMADE CONCOCTIONS RATHER THAN THE RE-PLATED

CHINESE TAKEOUT I HAD **PREVIOUSLY BEEN SERVING.**

ABOUT A YEAR INTO MY FORAY AS NEW YORK CITY DESIGNER-CUM-HOSTESS, I WAS INVITED TO DINNER BY ONE OF MY BEST CLIENTS, A WOMAN NAMED KARIN.

SHE WAS A POWERFUL AND BEAUTIFUL MEDIA EXECUTIVE, AND I WAS EXCITED TO BE WELCOMED INTO HER VERY EXCLUSIVE CLIQUE. I BOUGHT MYSELF A BRAND NEW BRIGHT PINK SWEATER FROM BENETTON

AND BROUGHT ALONG THE BEST BOTTLE OF WINE I COULD AFFORD.

WHEN KARIN'S HUSBAND OPENED THE DOOR TO THEIR DOWNTOWN LOFT,

I FELT AS IF I HAD MOMENTARILY LEFT THE PLANET.

THE LIGHTS IN THE APARTMENT
GLISTENED LIKE LITTLE STARS, AND THE
CLINK-CLINK OF THE CRYSTAL GLASSES
MADE IT SEEM AS IF ALL OF THE STARS
WERE BLINKING.
I LOOKED ALL AROUND AND SAW TALL,
SKINNY WOMEN IN SLEEVELESS BLACK
DRESSES
AND SINUOUS UPDOS
AND FELT
DULL AND LUMPY IN COMPARISON.
AND THE FOOD!
THERE WAS A TABLE A MILE WIDE PILED
HIGH WITH GLASSES AND BOWLS AND
PLATTERS OF THE MOST GLAMOROUS HORS
D'OEUVRES
I HAD EVER SEEN.

THERE
WERE
THICK
PÂTÉS,
COCKTAILS
THE
COLOR
OF
MY
SWEATER,
AND
SHRIMPS
THE
SIZE
OF
LOBSTERS.
I DIDN'T
KNOW
HOW
TO
ENTER
INTO
THIS
FOREIGN
WORLD
AND
STOOD
PARALYZED
NEXT
TO
THE
PUNCH.

SEEING MY DISMAY, KARIN CAME OVER, WRAPPED HER ARM AROUND MY SHOULDERS, AND INTRODUCED ME TO AN EDITOR FRIEND OF HERS. HER GRACE EASED MY INSECURITY, AND I TRIED TO AVOID EMBARRASSING HER WITH MY AWKWARDNESS AND NAIVETÉ.

AFTER THAT NIGHT, I RETHOUGHT MY OWN HOSTESSING EFFORTS AND VOWED THAT FROM THEN ON, I WOULD ENTERTAIN WITH A BIT MORE ELEGANCE AND SAVOIR FAIRE.

AND FOR THE MOST PART, I HAVE.
I STILL ENTERTAIN OFTEN, BUT

I HAVE LONG SINCE MOVED OUT OF
THE FOURTH-FLOOR WALK-UP. NOW,
GUESTS WALK DOWNSTAIRS
INTO MY LIVING ROOM.

ONE RECENT DECEMBER, I HAD AN END-OF-SEMESTER PARTY AT MY HOUSE FOR MY DESIGN STUDENTS AND FRIENDS AND SPENT THE AFTERNOON HAPPILY ARRANGING, PREPARING, AND ORGANIZING.

WHILE LOOKING OVER EVERYTHING I HAD SET UP, I STARTED WORRYING THAT I DIDN'T HAVE ENOUGH FOOD.

THE PRESENTATION LOOKED AMISS, AND I DECIDED THAT I DIDN'T HAVE THE RIGHT AMOUNT OF CHEESE.

WITH AN HOUR TO GO BEFORE THE SOIRÉE WAS SCHEDULED TO BEGIN,

I CALCULATED HOW MUCH TIME I NEEDED TO TREK TO THE MARKET, BUY MORE CHEESE,

AND RETURN HOME WITH ENOUGH TIME TO FINISH GETTING READY. I ESTIMATED THAT IF I RAN, I COULD JUST ABOUT DO IT.

IT WAS NEARLY DARK AS I RUSHED OUT,

AND I RACED THROUGH THE STORE BARELY LOOKING AT WHAT I WAS BUYING.

I LOADED UP MY CART AND CHOSE THE SHORTEST LINE.

I FRETFULLY ROCKED BACK AND FORTH WAITING MY TURN. THE WOMAN AHEAD OF ME SEEMED TO BE ON HER WAY OUT, BUT WHEN SHE GAVE THE CASHIER HER CREDIT CARD, IT DIDN'T GO THROUGH.

SHE ASKED THE CASHIER TO TRY IT AGAIN. AND AGAIN, IT DIDN'T WORK.

ANXIOUS AND IMPATIENT, I IMAGINED MYSELF AS GEORGE COSTANZA PUSHING HER OUT OF THE WAY WHILE YELLING

"FIRE!"

I LOUDLY SIGHED AND DID MY "INNER EYE ROLL." THE WOMAN TRIED ANOTHER CARD, BUT IT TOO WOULDN'T GO THROUGH. I GLANCED AT MY WATCH.

THE CASHIER ASKED HER IF SHE WANTED TO PAY WITH CASH, AND SHE EXAMINED HER WALLET. SHE SHOOK HER HEAD—NO, SHE DIDN'T HAVE ENOUGH MONEY; SHE APOLOGIZED AND WALKED OUT.

FINALLY, AT LONG LAST, *MY TURN!*

AS I PUT THE COPIOUS PACKAGES OF CHEESE ON THE CONVEYER BELT, I ASKED THE CASHIER WHAT THE WOMAN HAD BEEN TRYING TO BUY. SHE POINTED TO A BAG OF POTATOES AT THE END OF THE COUNTER. THE WOMAN HAD BEEN TRYING TO BUY A

BAG OF POTATOES.

HERE I WAS, ANXIOUSLY AND OBNOXIOUSLY TRYING TO PROVE WHO KNOWS WHAT BY PURCHASING LUDICROUS AMOUNTS OF CHEESE, AND THE WOMAN IN FRONT OF ME

DIDN'T HAVE ENOUGH MONEY TO BUY A THREE-POUND BAG OF POTATOES.

I STOOD RED-FACED AS I PAID FOR MY PURCHASES,
AND WHEN I WAS FINISHED, I HURRIED OUTSIDE TO
TRY TO FIND THE WOMAN.

BUT SHE WAS GONE.

IT WAS NOW COMPLETELY DARK OUTSIDE,
AND I WALKED BACK HOME SLOWLY.

I CARRIED THE CHEESE CLOSE TO MY CHEST AND MY EYES BURNED IN THE BITTER WIND.

WHEN I GOT HOME,
I PUT THE CHEESE
ON A PRETTY PLATTER AND FELT
THE

SMALLNESS

OF

MY

SPIRIT

AS I WAITED FOR MY GUESTS
TO ARRIVE.

LET IT BE

LET IT BE

Name an iconic song, and I can tell you everything that was occurring in my life at the time it was popular: when Meat Loaf's "Paradise by the Dashboard Light" was on the airwaves, I could be found in the front seat of Steven Bimini's bronze Pinto, a hot and sweaty youngster wearing white shorts, a YES T-shirt, and yellow flip-flops; my legs were covered in a summer's worth of mosquito bites, and I puffed on contraband cigarettes while arguing about the effectiveness of Jimmy Carter's cabinet.

Led Zeppelin's "Kashmir" has me at Eric Matthew's pool party, his poodle drunk on bad beer and running

IN MAD CIRCLES AROUND THE BACKYARD
WHILE I TRIED TO CONVINCE MYSELF
THAT THE "I AM BEGINNING TO" ANSWER
MY BOYFRIEND GAVE TO THE POINTED
QUESTION — "DO YOU LOVE ME?" — WAS
AN ACCEPTABLE RESPONSE. CUT TO
FLEETWOOD MAC'S "LANDSLIDE," AND I AM
BACK IN THE JOHN GLENN HIGH SCHOOL
CAFETERIA FOR MY JUNIOR PROM, CLAD
IN A PALE YELLOW LAURA ASHLEY-ESQUE

FORMAL DRESS, LOOKING UP AT A CEILING
COVERED IN TINFOIL TO MATCH THE PROM
THEME AND STEVIE NICKS' LYRICS
"OH, MIRROR IN THE SKY / WHAT IS LOVE?"

DURING THE SUMMER OF ORLEANS'
"DANCE WITH ME," I FELL IN LOVE WITH
A BOY OF 18 — THE OUTFIT I REMEMBER
WEARING AT THE TIME CONSISTED OF
AN ORANGE-AND-WHITE-STRIPED TUBE

TOP, GAUZY WHITE CULOTTES, AND AN
ARMFUL OF PLASTIC ORANGE BRACELETS.
MY PARENTS GOT DIVORCED WHEN THE
BEATLES' "LET IT BE" TOPPED THE CHARTS,
AND MY FAVORITE ACCESSORY WAS A PAIR
OF WHITE KNEE-HIGH PLASTIC BOOTS.
THE SUMMER AFTER MY COLLEGE
GRADUATION WAS DEFINED BY THE POLICE
ALBUM SYNCHRONICITY, DAVID BOWIE'S
LET'S DANCE, AND MY NEW TOWER RECORDS

T-SHIRT WITH CUTOFF SLEEVES.

MUSIC HAS BEEN AN OMNIPRESENT
MARKER IN MY LIFE; WHEN SOMEONE
EVEN CASUALLY MENTIONS A TUNE, OR
WHEN I HEAR THE FIRST CHORDS OF A
SONG, A CASCADE OF IMAGES AND SENSORY
PERCEPTIONS FILLS MY MIND WITH A
POTENCY UNLIKE THAT OF ANY OTHER
STIMULUS.

THESE SENSORY RECOLLECTIONS ARE FROZEN IN TIME — I HAVE BUT A SCANT MEMORY OF WHAT MIGHT HAVE COME BEFORE OR AFTER, AND I FIND THAT I CAN'T RECALL ANY OTHER OUTFITS, MEALS, OR PARTIES WITH THE SAME PRECISION WHEN I DON'T HAVE THE BENEFIT OF MY MENTAL MUSICAL NOTATION. TIME SLOWS AND THEN STOPS AS THIS VISCERAL SCULPTURE OF TIME PAST PUSHES FORTH, REPLETE WITH A SENSE OF TOUCH AND SMELL AND YEARNING AND YOUTH. THE MUSIC IS AS MUCH A PART OF THE MEMORY AS THE MEMORY IS OF MY IDENTITY.

WHAT IS IT ABOUT MUSIC THAT PROVIDES THIS SHORTCUT TO THE MINUTIAE OF BOTH OUR COLLECTIVE AND INDIVIDUAL HISTORIES? DR. OLIVER SACKS, THE WELL-KNOWN NEUROLOGIST WHO'S SPENT HIS career exploring the often mysterious workings of the mind, has long been intrigued with the indelible impression that music makes on our synapses. Encephalitis erased the memory of one of his patients, who nevertheless was still able to play and conduct music — though he couldn't remember doing so afterwards. After a brain injury, another patient was rendered unable to speak or comprehend words, yet was still capable of singing.

In an article for *The Washington Post*, journalist Shankar Vedantam examined research into music's connection to memory and the brain: "McGill scientist Robert Zatorre once hypothesized that because music

IS ABSTRACT, IT MUST ACTIVATE PARTS
OF THE BRAIN THAT PROCESS ABSTRACT
IDEAS... BUT WHEN ZATORRE ASKED
PEOPLE TO LISTEN TO THEIR FAVORITE
PIECES OF MUSIC AS HE RAN BRAIN
SCANS ON THEM... HE FOUND THAT MUSIC
ACTIVATED VERY ANCIENT PARTS OF
THE BRAIN."

WHAT IS FUNDAMENTALLY INTERESTING

ABOUT THIS IS THAT THERE SEEMS TO
BE A SYNCHRONICITY IN THE RELATIONSHIP
BETWEEN MUSIC AND MEMORY, BOTH OF
WHICH STIMULATE THE TEMPORAL LOBES
OF THE BRAIN. ACCORDING TO SCIENCE
WRITER WILLIAM J. CROMIE, "CERTAIN
TYPES OF MUSIC MAY ACTIVATE THE
TEMPORAL LOBES AND HELP THEM LEARN,
PROCESS, AND REMEMBER INFORMATION.
MUSIC OPENS NEW PATHWAYS INTO

THE MIND. ABSTRACT REASONING AND CONCEPTUALIZATION ARE ENHANCED BY MUSICAL ACTIVITIES, AND MUSIC ALSO CREATES A CONNECTION BETWEEN THE TWO HEMISPHERES OF THE BRAIN."

BUT THE BRAIN ONLY REMEMBERS THAT INFORMATION THAT IS "HOOKED" TO EMOTIONS. MUSIC ESSENTIALLY INCREASES OUR ATTENTION TO SOUNDS, TIMING,

AND PERCEPTION, AND ENHANCES MEMORY BY ATTACHING EMOTIONAL CONTEXT TO AN EVENT AND ACTIVATING MULTIPLE MEMORY PATHWAYS. AND BECAUSE COGNITIVE DEVELOPMENT, PHYSICAL DEVELOPMENT, AND EMOTIONS ARE ALL INTERTWINED, ALL BRAIN SYSTEMS ARE AFFECTED BY MUSIC. IT IS REMARKABLE TO ME THAT BECAUSE OF THIS INHERENT MULTIFACETED DEPENDENCY, MUSIC

ACTUALLY HELPS US TO REMEMBER AN
EXPERIENCE BETTER.

RECENTLY, I WAS IN A KARAOKE BAR AND
WATCHED AS MY FRIENDS BELTED OUT,
IN GRAND TRADITION, THE GREATEST HITS
OF THE '80s. WE ENJOYED A ROUSING
VERSION OF PAT BENATAR'S "HIT ME
WITH YOUR BEST SHOT," AN ENTERTAINING
TAKE ON DURAN DURAN'S "RIO," AND

A BAR-WIDE SINGALONG TO CULTURE
CLUB'S "DO YOU REALLY WANT TO HURT
ME." AFTER HOURS OF MY FRIENDS
URGING ME TO JOIN THE PERFORMERS,
I FINALLY AGREED TO BELT ONE OUT —
WITH CERTAIN CONDITIONS: I WOULD
CHOOSE A SONG THAT WASN'T FROM
THE '80s AND THAT I LOVED WITH
ALL MY HEART.

As I scoured through the voluminous catalog, I stopped with assurance when I saw the listing for the Beatles' "Let It Be." This was a song I could do! This was a song that would certainly prevent me from looking like an idiot. I sauntered up to the stage, hubris in hand. As I dramatically fiddled with the microphone, I realized I forgot my glasses and couldn't read the lyrics on the karaoke screen. But I brushed aside my worries when I remembered that this song was so embedded in my personal history, I could likely sing it backwards.

After the first stanza, I discovered I was wrong. While I could remember exactly what I was wearing, thinking,

DREAMING, AND DRINKING THE MOMENT "LET IT BE" FIRST DEBUTED, I HAD ABSOLUTELY NO IDEA WHAT THE ACTUAL LYRICS WERE. WHAT WAS THE LINE AFTER "AND IN MY HOUR OF DARKNESS, SHE IS STANDING RIGHT IN FRONT OF ME"? WAS IT "THERE WILL BE AN ANSWER, LET IT BE," OR "WHISPER WORDS OF WISDOM, LET IT BE"? I HAD ABSOLUTELY, POSITIVELY NO IDEA.

MY FRIENDS LAUGHED AS I FUMBLED, AND I COULD SEE THEY THOUGHT I WAS JUST A RELUCTANT PERFORMER. BUT I KNEW BETTER. WHILE THE SONG HELPED CRYSTALLIZE MY MEMORIES, THE MEMORIES OBLITERATED THE ACTUAL CONTENT OF THE SONG. AS THE CROWD ROARED WITH HYSTERIA, I SHEEPISHLY SMILED AS I PROCEEDED TO MAKE UP MY OWN WORDS. AND THEN I REALIZED THAT UNLIKE MY MEMORY OF THE LYRICS, I WOULD NEVER,

EVER BE able TO FORGET THIS MOMENT.

IF THAT HADN'T HAPPENED

I often say that there are only three things that I know. I know what I know: that I am a woman, that I am left-handed, and I am clumsy. I also know what I don't know: I can't speak a foreign language, I will never be a

I will never be a brain surgeon, and I will never play the piano like Glenn Gould.

But What keeps me up late at night, and constantly gives me reason to fret, is this:

I don't know what

I dont know, there are universes of things out there ideas, philosophies, songs, subtleties facts, emotions that exist, but of which I am totally and thoroughly unaware. This makes me very uncomfortable. I find that the only way to find out the fuller extent of what I don't know is FOR SOMEONE to tell me,

teach me

OR SHOW ME, and then open my eyes to this

BIT OF INFORMATION,

Knowledge, or life experience that I, sadly, never before considered. AFTERWARD,

I find something odd happens. I find that what I have just learned is suddenly everywhere: on billboards or in the newspaper or SMACK!

Right in front of me, and I can't help but shake my head and speculate how and why I never saw or knew this particular thing before. And I begin to wonder if I could be any DIFFERENT, SMARTER, OR MORE INTERESTING had I discovered it when everyone else in the world found out about this particular obvious thing. I have been thinking a lot about these first discoveries and also those chance encounters:

those
elusive
happenstances
that often lead
to defining
moments in our
lives.

But what if one of those defining experiences never occurred?

What if some-thing wonder-ful, something that we have come to depend on, that serendipitous bit of luck that had provided us with a big break or a big deal of the BIG TIME, what if it never happened? one of those "if I hadn't been eating a gigantic McDonald's breakfast on the 7am.

flight to Vancouver in the middle seat, I wouldn't have apologized to the beautiful, elegant woman sitting next to me on the plane, and we wouldn't have started talking and I wouldn't have found out she was an important editor of a cool design magazine and we wouldn't have become friends and so on and so on" type of moments.

I call this "SIX degrees of serendipity." The quintessential recognition, that "if that didn't happen then that wouldn't have happened and then that would n't have

HAPPENED AND WE wouldn't have ended up right here, right now, in this way"

On the other hand, what if we could turn back time and eliminate the bad haircut, the bad fight, the bad boyfriend? Would we simply do what Freud suggested and inevitably recreate the previous traumatic experience

in
the

altruistic
attempt to
alter the

original
course

?

I think the reason we
"recreate" experiences or
situations to try to
change the outcome
on the second go
is because we
regret what the original
experience did to us. That particular defining moment in our
lives was not as fortuitous as,
say, sitting next to a cool editor
on an airplane. It is more of a,
"well, if I wasn't treated so badly
at that time, then
I wouldn't feel
so worthless now and I
wouldn't feel so empty
and hopeless." Our
recreative urge be-
comes a wish to defy history—
to defy how we've ended up.

I once read that the definition of insanity is doing the same thing over and over and expecting different results. I fundamentally disagree with this idea. I think that doing the same thing over and over and expecting different results IS the definition of hope. We might keep making mistakes, but the struggle gives us a sense of EMPATHY AND CONNECTIVITY that we would not experience otherwise. I believe this empathy improves our ability to see the unseen and to better know the unknown.

Lives are shaped by chance encounters and by discovering things that we don't know that we don't know. The arc of a life is a circuitous one. You never know who you may sit next to on a plane. In the grand scheme of things, EVERYTHING WE do is an experiment the outcome of which is unknown.

You never know when a typical

life will be
anything but,
and you
won't know
if you
are re-
writing
history,
or rewrit-
ing the
future,
until
the
writing
is
Complete.

This, just this,
I am
comfortable
not knowing.

PICK ONE

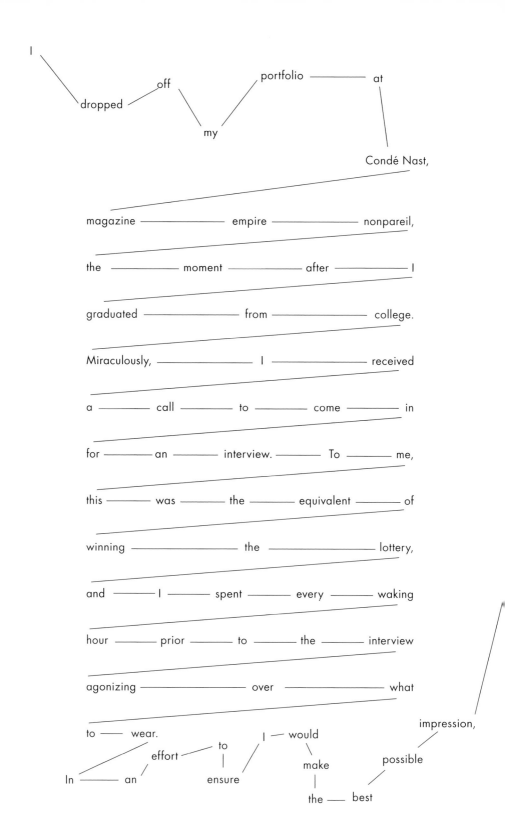

I dropped off my portfolio at Condé Nast, magazine empire nonpareil, the moment after I graduated from college. Miraculously, I received a call to come in for an interview. To me, this was the equivalent of winning the lottery, and I spent every waking hour prior to the interview agonizing over what to wear. In an effort to ensure I would make the best possible impression,

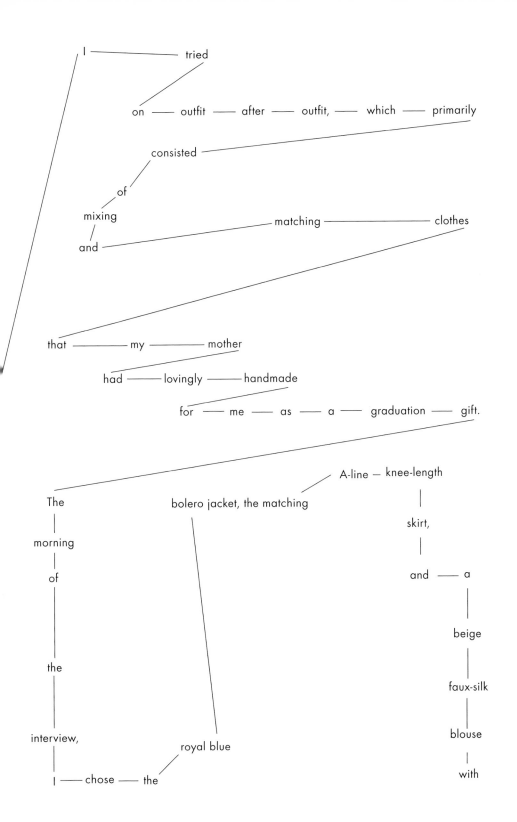

I tried
on outfit after outfit, which primarily
consisted
of
mixing matching clothes
and
that my mother
had lovingly handmade
for me as a graduation gift.
The A-line — knee-length
bolero jacket, the matching skirt,
morning and a
of beige
the faux-silk
interview, blouse
I chose the royal blue with

127

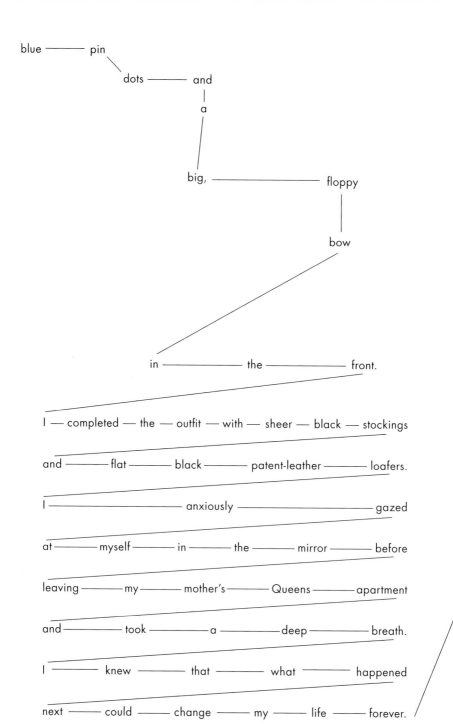

blue —— pin

dots —— and

a

big, —————— floppy

bow

in ———— the ———— front.

I — completed — the — outfit — with — sheer — black — stockings

and ——— flat ——— black ——— patent-leather ——— loafers.

I ————————— anxiously ————————— gazed

at ——— myself ——— in ——— the ——— mirror ——— before

leaving ——— my ——— mother's ——— Queens ——— apartment

and ——— took ——— a ——— deep ——— breath.

I ——— knew ——— that ——— what ——— happened

next ——— could ——— change ——— my ——— life ——— forever.

As — I — sat — on — the — cramped,
balmy — express — bus — into — Manhattan,
I — fantasized — befriending — the — human — resources — director,
being — invited — up — to — meet — the — design — director — of — *Vogue*,
Vanity — *Fair*, — or — *Glamour*, — getting — hired — as
his — or — her — crackerjack — assistant,
working — late — nights — and — weekends,
cavorting — with — glamorous — editors
and — art — directors — and — designers, — and,
of — course, — spending — my — entire — career
being — fabulously — successful — at — what — I
considered — to — be — the — best — magazine — company — in — the
whole
wide
world.

I — exited — the — bus — at — 42nd — Street — and — Madison — Avenue

and — skipped — toward — the — Condé — Nast — building, — faux-silk

bow — billowing — in — the — breeze, — faux-leather — portfolio — banging

against — my — legs, — when — the — unthinkable — happened.

I tripped. I toppled so — hard and so

fast that — three passersby — came to

help me. — As they asked me if I was okay,

I felt my — stinging knee and — burning face

and knew — without looking:

I had an — ugly bruise on my

leg and a — vicious tear up my stockings.

I didn't have —— time to change my hose, but realized —— that both my skirt and —— the tactical —— placement of my portfolio —— could mask the bruise. —— I lumbered on and made it to —— my appointment on time. —— When I met the human resources director, I was mesmerized. —— She was unlike any —— woman –I had ever encountered. She was cool, —— elegant, —— and alluring in her pale yellow sleeveless shift. —— She had the —— thinnest arms —— I had ever seen, and the —— biggest office I had ever been in. —— She invited me to sit down, —— and I complied. —— As I tumbled back into the —— overstuffed orange chair, —— I felt the hole in my stockings —— widen and prayed that she didn't —— hear the ripping sound. —— She quickly looked through my portfolio without uttering a syllable, —— and when she was finished, she shut it with a thud. —— She looked me up — and —— down, and we had —— the following —— conversation:

She:
So. What kind
of design do
you want to
do? —————— Me:
Excuse me?

She:
What kind of
design do you
want to do? / Me:
Kind of design?

She:
[Said with a furrowed
brow.] Yes.

Me:
Er ... um ... I
think I would like
to do any kind of
design....

She:
You can't do
any kind of
design. You
have to pick. ————— Me:
Pick?

She:
[Said with a very furrowed
brow.] Yes. You have to pick. You
have to pick editorial design or
promotional design or advertising or custom publishing. You
must choose one.

I sat there for a moment and thought to myself:
Well, I really want to say "editorial," but maybe
I am not good enough, and though I don't know
what custom publishing and promotional design
are, I will say "promotional." But really I would
happily sweep the floors if they want me to. . . .

Finally, I cleared my throat and said:
Promotional?

And then I couldn't help myself. —————— I continued talking.

Me:
But I would do
anything. Anything.
Anything you need. —————— And then there was silence.

And she responded:
Well. Yes, then. I see.

And with that, —— she —————— sighed and made —— one sweeping —— gesture for me to —— take —— my —— portfolio back. I looked —— at her —— and picked it up. Though she —————— said she would be in touch, —————— I —————— knew that I was not going to —————— hear from —————— her, and I never, —————— ever did. I made some small —————— talk as —————— I was escorted out; —— I —————— recall asking her how long —————— she had —— been at Condé Nast, —————— and I remember her replying "12 years" —————— with the slightest —————— clip in her voice.

Several months later, —————— in a moment of aberrant —————— fearlessness, I got up my —— nerve and called her, —————— but the person who —————— answered the phone told me she —— no longer worked there. By then —— I —————— had gotten my first job as a —————— "traffic girl" at a fledgling cable —————— magazine and —————— worked late —— nights and weekends and —————— cavorted with the editors, —————— art directors, and designers, and, of course, —— I didn't spend the rest of my career there. But when I worked there, — I joyfully learned about editorial design, promotional — design, — advertising, — and — even custom — publishing. — I — realized — how — much — I did — know — and — how — much — I — didn't — know, and —— embarked —— upon —— what —— has become a —— lifelong journey in —————— learning about — the — abundant — and — bewitching specialties — in — the — marvelous — discipline that — is — known — as — graphic — design.

Twenty-five years after ——— that decisive day,

I've come to — the realization ——— that my

ill-fated interview — did indeed ——— impact the

rest —— of my life, — just not in the way I intended

it to. But this —— is ——— likely the most

interesting ——— thing about — possibilities:

There is always

something new to dream of and

always different dreams to choose.

And you ——————— don't

have to pick just one.

ECONOMY FOAM

I LIVE IN NEW YORK CITY –
ON THE ISLAND OF MANHATTAN. FOR
MANY OF US WHO LIVE IN THIS BOIS-
TEROUS, BOSSY, AND BUSTLING TOWN,
WE'VE COME TO BELIEVE WITH
UNWAVERING CERTAINTY THAT WE
LIVE IN THE FINEST PLACE IN THE
WORLD, A CITY FILLED WITH THE
BEST OF EVERYTHING. AND
THE BIGGEST OPPORTUNITIES.
AND IF YOU CAN MAKE IT HERE,
YADDA YADDA YADDA.

SUFFICE IT TO SAY
THAT AFTER 48 YEARS OF LIFE AS A
NATIVE NEWYORKER, I HAVE BE-
COME USED TO THE UNUSUAL- OR
WHAT IS CONSIDERED RATHER
USUAL HERE: PEOPLE SLEEPING IN
THE STREETS, AMPUTEES BEGGING
IN THE SUBWAYS, CELEBRITIES
STANDING AT ATMs, limousines
PARKED IN FRONT OF DIVE BARS.
EVERYTHING IS ACCEPTABLE
IN NYC AND MOST OF US LIKE
IT THIS WAY.

THE VISUAL LAND-
SCAPE IN MANHATTAN IS ONE OF
THE RICHEST IN THE WORLD. THE
SENSORY PHANTASMAGORIA TO
BE FOUND HERE INCLUDES
THE LED SIGNS ON 42nd STREET,
THE SIMPLE HANDMADE SIGNS
DISPLAYED BY FAMILY-RUN
BUSINESSES. THE SOFT-PORN
CALVIN KLEIN POSTERS TOWER-
ING OVER HOUSTON STREET,
THE CONSTANTLY TALLYING
U.S. DEBT METER THAT
COMPUTES THE HUNDREDS OF
THOUSANDS OF DOLLARS
APPORTIONED TO INDIVIDUAL
HOUSEHOLDS. AND THE WITTY
AND NOW VERNACULAR
PUBLIC THEATER POSTERS
WE have RELISHED
SINCE THE MID-'90s.

MY FAVORITE SIGN IS ONE THAT I HAVE BEEN OGLING FOR YEARS - AS IS MY HABIT. I WILL PURPOSELY TAKE CAB ROUTES JUST TO SEE SOME OF MY FAVORITE VISUAL LANDMARKS: TIBOR KALMAN'S STUPID ASKEW CLOCK ATOP THE RED SQUARE APARTMENT BUILDING, KEITH HARING'S "CRACK IS WACK" MURAL OFF OF THE HARLEM RIVER DRIVE, OR THE POLKA-DOTTED CEMENT MIXERS LINING THE EAST RIVER. I LOVE TO LOOK AT THE JOHN J. HARVEY FIREBOAT ANCHORED OFF OF CHELSEA PIERS, AND THE '70s-STYLE DECAL IN THE WINDOW OF A BROWNSTONE ON 13TH STREET, SHOWING A POT OF GOLD AT THE END OF A RAINBOW (!)

THAT STICKER HAS BEEN THERE AS LONG AS I'VE BEEN IN THE CITY, AND EVERY TIME I PASS IT, I CAN'T HELP BUT WONDER IF THE APARTMENT HAS BEEN INHABITED BY ONE FAMILY THIS ENTIRE TIME, OR IF EVERY NEW TENANT THERE HAS SIMPLY KEPT IT IN PLACE, BECAUSE, WELL, IT MAKES THEM SMILE, TOO.

I OFTEN RITUALIZE
MY VIEWINGS:
EVERY YEAR DURING GAY
PRIDE WEEK, I MAKE SURE TO
GET A GOOD LOOK AT THE
EMPIRE STATE BUILDING WHEN
IT'S AWASH IN LAVENDER
LIGHTS. WHENEVER I GO TO
MADISON SQUARE GARDEN,
I LINGER TO EXAMINE THE
ENGRAVED TILES OF ANONYMOUS
SPORTS FANS DEDICATING THE
SMALL RECTANGULAR SPACES
TO LOVED ONES OR SOME PERSONAL
PURPOSE. ON MY DAILY WALK
PAST THE LITTLE CHURCH ON
31st STREET, I HOPE TO FIND
NEW HANDWRITTEN MESSAGES
OFFERING INSPIRATION OR AN
ADMONITION TO JUST STOP
BEING RIDICULOUS
FOR A DAY.

MY FAVORITE SIGN
GRACED THE INTERSECTION
OF ALLEN AND HOUSTON

STREETS FOR MANY YEARS.
THE WRITING ON IT WAS
IN A BOLD UPPERCASE AND
LOWERCASE SCRIPT THAT
HAD BEEN HAND-PAINTED
DECADES AGO. THE TYPE
WAS HUGE — THE SIGN
WAS THE LENGTH OF THE
BUILDING'S SIDE, SO YOU COULD
SEE IT ALONG A STRETCH OF
ALLEN STREET, AND THE LET-
TERS WERE BLACK ON A WHITE
BACKGROUND.
    THE SIGN STATED SIMPLY:
"ECONOMY FOAM"

I WAS OBSESSED WITH THE
MESSAGE FOR YEARS— NOT
ONLY BECAUSE IT WAS SIMPLE
AND HEARTBREAKINGLY BEAU-
TIFUL, BUT BECAUSE IT
WAS SO ODD. WHO KNEW
THERE WERE GRADES OF
FOAM? LIKE THE VARIED SE-
LECTION FOR MILK OR AIR-
LINE TICKETS OR AMERICAN
APPAREL T-SHIRT SIZES, I
IMAGINED THAT THERE WAS
A PREMIUM FOAM AND A SUPER-
PREMIUM FOAM AND PERHAPS
EVEN AN ULTRA-PREMIUM FOAM.

WHO KNEW THIS TYPE OF CHOICE COULD EXIST?

DURING ONE VISIT TO THE
EAST VILLAGE, I WALKED BY
THE ECONOMY FOAM BUILD-
ING, AND TO MY HORROR,
THE SIGN WAS GONE. AP-
PARENTLY, THE STRUCTURE
WAS COMING DOWN, AND
ECONOMY FOAM HAD VACATED.
I WAS INCONSOLABLE. I
HAD NO VISUAL EVIDENCE
OF THIS SIGN OTHER THAN
WHAT WAS ETCHED IN MY
MIND, AND NOW THAT IT WAS
GONE, I WORRIED
THAT IT WOULD FADE
FOREVER FROM MY
PERSONAL VISUAL
LANDSCAPE.

WELL, I NEEDN'T HAVE
WORRIED. ECONOMY FOAM
IS NOW BACK AT THE
INTERSECTION OF ALLEN
AND HOUSTON STREETS—
BUT IN TRUE NEW YORK
FASHION, THE LOGO HAS
BEEN REDESIGNED.

THE MESSAGE IS STILL "ECONOMY FOAM," BUT EVERYTHING ELSE COULDN'T BE MORE DIFFERENT. THE NAME IS NOW IN A SANS-SERIF, ALL-LOWERCASE FONT. THE TYPE IS WHITE ON A FOREST-GREEN BACK-GROUND — AND REMINDS ME OF SOMETHING YOU WOULD SEE ON PRODUCTS IN UPSCALE SHOPS LIKE MOSS OR CONRAN'S. I WAS BEWILDERED:

HOW STRONG COULD THE MARKET FOR "ECONOMY FOAM" BE?

I GOT AN INKLING DURING A TRIP TO WISCONSIN, WHEN I VISITED APPLETON, A QUAINT, MIDWESTERN TOWN WITH LOTS OF STRIP MALLS, WAL-MARTS, AND COSTCO'S. THE LIFESTYLE IN THE AREA SEEMED TO BE VERY FAMILY ORIENTED: MOMS SCREEN THE KIDS' MOVIES BEFORE THEY LET THEIR CHILDREN SEE THEM, CHURCHES ARE PACKED ON SUNDAYS, AND NOBODY EVER WEARS ALL BLACK.

ON MY
SOJOURN TO
THE ONLY STARBUCKS
IN APPLETON, I TOOK IN
THIS NEW VISUAL SETTING
AND THERE, PARKED IN FRONT
OF JAKE'S SUBS, RIGHT
NEXT TO THE STARBUCKS,
WAS A COMMERCIAL VAN
WITH A LOGO ON THE SIDE
FOR "TAILORED FOAM".
NOT ECONOMY, NOT PREMIUM,
OR ULTRA-PREMIUM, BUT
TAILORED. THE EMBLEM
WAS BEAUTIFULLY DESIGNED,
VERY CONFIDENT AND
PROUD- THE MARK OF A
SUCCESSFUL-LOOKING BUSINESS.
AND I COULDN'T
HELP BUT LAUGH AS I
REALIZED THAT NO MATTER
WHERE YOU ARE IN THE WORLD
THERE IS ALWAYS SOMETHING
TO LOOK AT THAT WILL
TEACH YOU SOMETHING,
CHANGE THE WAY YOU
THINK, OR JUST OPEN
YOUR MIND TO POSSIBILITIES
YOU MAY NOT HAVE
CONSIDERED BEFORE.

NECESSARY OBJECTS

As far back

as I can

remember, I've

collected things.

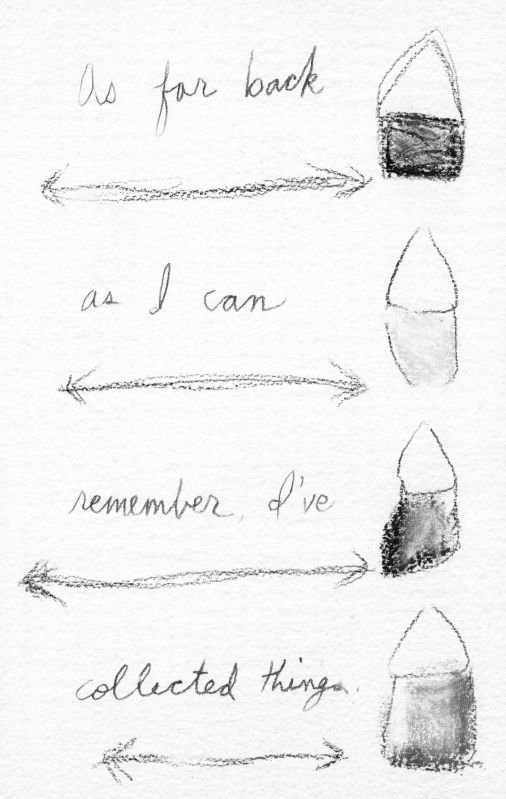

This propensity was already in
full bloom when I was about
five years old: If
someone gave me a
gift of candy,

rather than eat it
immediately — as my younger
brother did — I secretly hid
it away in an old pocketbook my
mother had given me to use when
I was playing dress-up. No one
knew I didn't eat any of the candy,

← - - - - - - - - - →

and after several months,
I amassed quite a collection
of lollipops, Sweet Tarts, Life
Savers, and NECCO Wafers. I
never consumed any of this sugary
stash; I was simply content to
admire my private treasure.

One day,
very mysteriously,
my pocketbook disappeared.

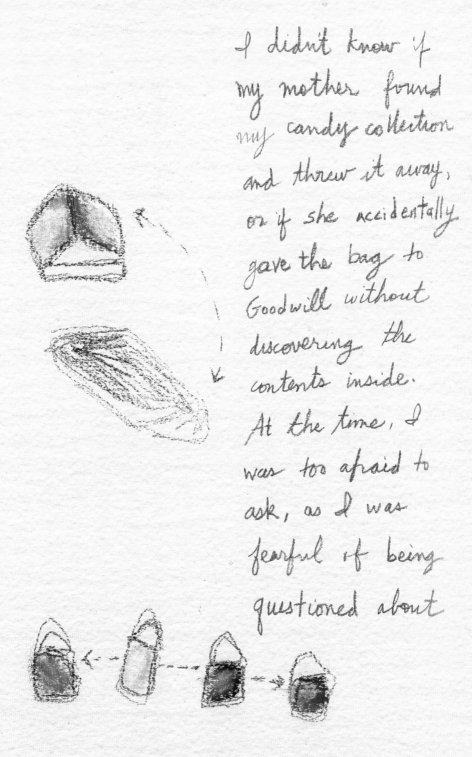

I didn't know if my mother found my candy collection and threw it away, or if she accidentally gave the bag to Goodwill without discovering the contents inside. At the time, I was too afraid to ask, as I was fearful of being questioned about

my strange pack-rat
behavior. When I
discovered the purse
was gone, my heart
broke. It wasn't
until 30 years
later that
I finally
asked my
mom

about the lost pocketbook.
She had absolutely no
recollection of it at all.
I will never, ever know
what happened to those hidden treats.

I still collect things,
but now the objects tend
to be items that are
more useful than sweets.
I feel blissfully content
when I open up my
kitchen closet and see
my shelves neatly
stocked with copious

←- - - - - - - - - - - - →
3 feet

quantities of paper
towels, tissue boxes, and
toilet paper. I am strangely
proud when I see all these
things, and I admire them
in the same way as I long
ago delighted in my
secret candy collection.

Whenever I open the closet door, I smile. I find these humble products to be beautiful in their simplicity — the perfectly round rolls of winter-white paper and the iconic boxes. Their loveliness, at least to me, is as real as their usefulness.

On contemplating my desire to maintain a large supply of household paper products, I have considered that it is more than just the search for psychological gratification that fuels my need for this abundance. Initially, I thought this cache gave me a profound sense of readiness and self-sufficiency — but now I feel that it goes even deeper than that: they make me feel safe.

In the book *Safe*: Design Takes on Risk, MoMA design curator Paola Antonelli writes, "Safety is an instinctive need that has guided human choices throughout history. Like love, it is a universal feeling, and as such, has inspired endless analytical thinking and motivated science, literature and art.

3 inches

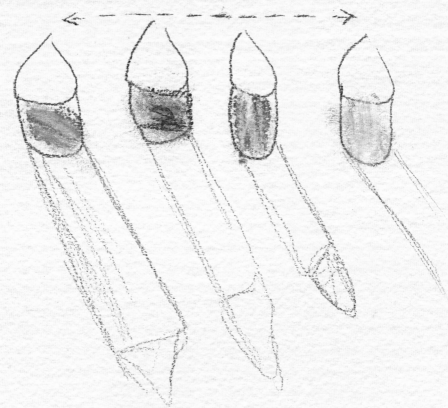

On our sleeves, we wear not
only our hearts, but also big red
panic buttons. As often happens
with basic tenets of human nature,
no definition of safety can be more
powerful than the ones that each of

us carries inside."

Much was written a few years ago about an odd gift that Martha Stewart gave out to the audience of her morning television show. In contrast to other celebrity hosts, who were giving away cars and exotic vacation packages, Stewart presented each member of her audience with a roll of toilet paper. "What a cheapskate," one blogger sniffed. I disagree. As I pondered the gift, I couldn't help but wonder if Stewart, like me, found security in maintaining a reserve of necessary objects in order to avoid the risk of running out. I wondered if she, like me, felt that having

an abundance of something small
helped her feel safe in an
unsafe world.

In fact,

the only
criticism I
could make

of this unusual offering was not of
the item itself, but of the quantity.

I am convinced that,
of all people, Martha
must know that rather
than a single roll of
toilet paper, a much,
much better gift
would have been
a pack of 36.

160

PEONIES

As a native
New Yorker,
I've spent countless stretches
of time roaming the streets of
Manhattan. Over the years,
I've developed a relationship
with places, monuments,
landmarks, and street signs.
I realize that certain of my
favorite pilgrimage sites, and
the feelings they evoke in me,
are clichéd; nevertheless,
I can't help but admire
the sadness and fury of
the Manhattan skyline or
bask in the glow of the bril-
liant lights enveloping the
Empire State Building.

I also get enormous pleasure
seeing and savoring things
I think of as "mine" — a '70s-
style decal in the window of
a townhouse that shows a
rainbow leading to a pot of
gold; a wooden owl on the
awning of a building on East
29th Street; a miniature
windmill on Hudson Street
I used to think was a helicop-
ter on its side; and the old
Economy Foam sign on Allen
Street in the Lower East Side.
These things, of course, are
not really mine, but somehow
I imagine I have a secret
relationship with them.
In my mind, they are not
really "things." They have
an existential gravitas that
is real, and they all have private lives and little souls.

My favorite thing to behold in
all of Manhattan used to be a
big bush of white peonies on
the street where I live. The

plant lived in a small messy garden in front of an apartment building that was rumored to have once been a crack house. Every year, in the middle of March, little buds would poke up through the thawing earth. Once they did, I would watch the daily drama of these peonies as they unfurled. First came the fringy black stems, next the leaves would turn green, then the stems would spurt forth tiny, perfectly round buds, and then, seemingly overnight, the buds would turn white and voilà! They would burst open into the most fantastically glamorous resplendence. It was magical and mysterious, and it made me very, very happy. Watching it year after year, I often wondered how the bush got there. Who planted it? Did it self-sow? I desperately wanted to know.

One day some years ago, while
walking my dogs, I bumped
into my neighbor Kathy, who
has lived on our block for 40
years. Kathy was out with her
dog, and as our pups frolicked
together on the sidewalk,
I realized we were in front
of the house with the peonies.
I asked her, "Do you know
who planted these flowers?"
She told me she did, and
related a story about a little
girl from the neighborhood
who was selling seeds to raise
money for her grade school.
Someone in the building
bought a package of seeds
and planted the entire pack
in front of the house. The little
girl wasn't so little anymore,
and she had moved away some
time ago, as did the person
who planted the seeds.
Together we nodded, admiring
their long-lasting handiwork,
and then we went our
separate ways.

Late one summer, walking home from work in a pink and purple August twilight, I realized that the peony bush was no longer there. It was gone. There wasn't a hole where the plant had been; there wasn't a splattering of dirt or debris. The bush simply disappeared. It was as if it had never been there at all, as if it hadn't been real.
I was devastated.

The nature of "what is real" is a confounding concept. Philosophers and scientists alike have attempted to define this, and to understand the nature of the consciousness that apprehends what is real.

Plato maintained that two distinct levels of reality exist: the visible world of sights and sounds that we live in, and the archetypal world populated by what he referred to as

"Forms" that stands above the visible universe and gives it meaning. Plato asserted that the "Forms of things" constitute the only essential existence, and that things as we experience them are only an appearance of reality. He believed that in our everyday perception, we suffer from the illusion that the things and objects around us constitute the ultimate reality. Furthermore, he argued that our ideas not only reveal our subjective inner states, but the true nature of reality itself.

So I had to wonder: Where were the peonies? How could they have disappeared without a trace? Could someone have been so cruel as to steal the bush and clean up after the theft? My mind raced. Could I put up a "Missing Peonies" poster? Were other people lamenting the loss of the flowers?

And I couldn't help but ponder in sadness: Were the peonies ever real?

On a subsequent Sunday, I was coming home from a last-minute holiday-shopping foray, my arms loaded with big bags of presents and wrapping paper. As I was making my way down the street, I passed the spot where my beloved peonies once resided. I stopped short. In a patch of dirt close to where the peonies had grown was a new bush of blooming white peonies. I couldn't believe it.

I approached the plant with delicacy, and once again, I was skeptical. This couldn't be happening, this couldn't possibly be real! I put down my bags and took off my gloves. I reached out to touch the peonies and suddenly realized: They weren't real. Someone had put a plastic peony plant close to where the real bush had been. One imaginative neighbor was commemorating the missing peonies, and this was the memorial. I smiled and suddenly felt hopeful that a fake peony bush could indeed be a very real testament to what is most real in our hearts.

LOST IN TRANSLATIONS

Recently, I spent a week in Tokyo observing Japanese consumers articulate their feelings about mouthwash and a potential new package design. It seems absurd, really, to describe my role in this qualitative market research as an observer; it is much more precise to say that I was a listener. I stood rapt with attention as a young woman translated into English what these unusually loyal mouthwash users were saying in Japanese. Her interpretations were remarkably creative, comprising such statements as "the packaging looks lonely" and "the design is like a fluffy painting." I couldn't help but wonder if her surprising pronouncements were the verbatim decoding of what was being said or the result of an imaginative reconstruction. I'll never know. Being in a country where the language and the alphabet were both foreign and unreadable reminded me forcefully of my reliance on language and reading to communicate and relate. The experience underscored how dependent I am on the ability to decipher signs in order to distinguish whether my destination is joyfully welcoming or dreadfully

最近、東京に一週間滞在した折、日本の消費者がマウスウォッシュや新しいパッケージ・デザインについて忌憚のない意見を述べるのを観察した。この質的市場調査における私の役割はオブザーバーというよりは、聞き役と言ったほうが正確だろう。私は、そのマウスウォッシュを使用している消費者が日本語で語った言葉を、通訳の若い女性が英語に翻訳するのを熱心に聞いていた。通訳の言葉はとても創造的で、「パッケージが寂しげだ」、「デザインはふわふわした絵のようだ」などの表現が繰り出された。そのため、通訳が次々繰り出すびっくりする表現が、発言者の一語一語の正確な通訳なのか、それとも通訳者が創造力を働かせて再構成したものなのかと考えずにはいられなかった。

答えを得ることはおそらくないだろう。言葉も文字も理解できない国にいることで、文字を読んだり、見たりして意思を伝えることは、結局、言語に頼らざるを得ないのだという状況を思い知らされた。この経験で、行くべく先が楽しく快適な場所なのか、それとも恐ろしく危険な場所なのかを区別し、確かに行くべきが先か分かっているのを再確認するのに、自分が記号、最近、東京に一週間滞在した折、日本の消費者がマウスウォッシュや新しいパッケージ・デ

me that I know where I am going. While in Tokyo, I was humbled by my utter disconnection from all these guideposts.

を述べるのを観察した。この質的市場調査における私の役割はオブザーバー

I have been thinking about the inadequacy of language and interpretation. What is language, really? Why is it that sounds have com

というほど、聞き役と言ったほうが正確だろう。私は、そのマウスウォッシュを使用している消費者

to embody meaning? How accurate are those meanings? These are basic questions of the philosophy of language. And language, like

が日本語で語った言葉

design, is a system of signs used to communicate. The act of communicating is a matter of letting other people know what we think

を、通訳の若い女性が英語に翻訳するのを熱心に聞いていた。通訳の言葉はとても創造的で、「パッケージが寂しげだ」、「デ

in many cases, what to think. The signs that make up language get their meaning

ザインはふわふわした絵のようだ」などの表現が繰り出された。そのため、通訳

from the ideas we associate with them and our collective agreement about these associations.

が次々繰り出すびっくりする表現が、発言者の一語一語の正確な通訳なのか、それとも通訳者が創造力を動かせて再構成したものなの

John Locke, the great British philosopher, believed that thought originates in experience—not in language. Ideas develop as the

と考えずにはいられなかった。

product of experience. And through this power of association, ideas are transformed into complex mental constructs like language.

答えを得ることはおそらくないだろう。言葉も文字も理解できない国にいることで、文字を読んだり、見たりして意思を伝えることは、結局

But language is a highly arbitrary and highly interpretive medium. Back when I was about 10 or 11 years old, I went

言語に頼らざるを得ないのだという状況を思い知らされた。この

through a particularly difficult phase in my life, when my behavior, in reflecting on it now, could be best described as characterized

経験で、行く先が楽しく快適な場所なのか、それとも恐ろしく危険な場所なのかを区別し、確かに行く先が分

y post-traumatic stress disorder. As a result of the disruption of my outer world, my inner

かっていると再確認するのに、自分が記号

world began to crumble, and I developed a bizarre speech

を読み取る能力にどれほど頼っているのかを裏付けするに至った。東京滞在中は、このような道標が全く分から

dysfunction. Whenever anyone asked me how I was doing, or what the weather was like, or any other innocuous question, I froze. I

ず屈辱的な思いをした。

couldn't answer.

私は、言葉と翻訳の不適合について考えている。実際のところ、言葉とは何だろうか。耳から入ってくる音

nasmuch as I thought I knew how I was doing or what the weather

が何らかの意味を具体化するのはなぜなのか。その意味はどれほど正確なのだろう。こうした問いは、言語哲学の基本的な疑

was like, I felt that I couldn't be absolutely sure. What if my idea about how I was doing wasn't real?

問である。言葉は、デザインのように、意思伝達

What if the weather was different somewhere else? As I tried to answer these benign questions,

に使われる記号の体系であり、意思伝達という行為は、自分の考え、または多くの

found that all I could muster were responses such as, "Well, maybe I am feeling well, but maybe I am not," or, "Maybe it is raining,

場合は考えるべき対象を他人に知らせることである。言葉を構成する記号は、私たちがそれに関連させる考えや考えに関連に

but maybe it is not." "Maybe or maybe not"

ついての集団的合意から意味を得る。

ecame my standard reply to any question, including what I wanted for dinner.

英国の偉大な哲学者、ジョン・ロックは、思考は、言葉ではなく、体験に発する、と考えていた。考えは

My mother and stepfather were horrified and angry at my inability to articulate an answer to the simplest

体験の所産として発達する。この関連付けの力を経て、考えは言葉のような複雑な精神的構築物に変質する。

of questions, and I was punished for my lack of conviction and clarity. But, for the life of me, I couldn't fathom at that time how anyone could be sure of anything. I preferred to be banished to my bedroom than to utter a phrase that contained a fixed belief on anything, including what I wanted for dessert.

Given that language is our primary tool for thinking, can we perceive or describe something without first having a linguistic boundary for it? And where does nuance fit in? What about ambiguity? The French philosopher Jacques Derrida stated that we inhabit "a world of signs without fault, without truth, and without origin." One of the central tenets of his philosophy is that "there is nothing outside the text." Derrida's philosophy is named deconstruction, an apt name, since its adherents seek to deconstruct the nature and meaning of language. Several phrases expressing this point of

が、言葉は非常に恣意的で解釈の余地の多い手段である。10歳、11歳ごろの私は、人生の中で特に難しい時期にあった。今から考えると、当時の私の行動は、心的外傷後ストレス障害と言えるだろう

ろ以外の世界が混乱した結果、内なる世界も崩れ始め、私には奇妙な言語障害が出始めた。私には返答が凍りついた。私は凍りついたのである。

自分の調子はどうだとか、お天気はどうかなどの他愛のない質問をされると、私は返答ができなかったのである。

について分かっていると考えれば考えるほど私には確信がなくなった。自分の具合についての考えが現実に即していない場合はどうなるのだろうか。どこか他の場所で天気が違う場合はどうだろうか。こうした悪意のない質問に答えるようとすると、私は、「そうねえ、気分はいいかもしれないし、悪いかもしれない」や「雨が降っているかもしれないし、降っていないかもしれないと答える

のが精一杯だった。夕食で何が食べたいかなどあらゆる質問に対して、「そうかもしれないし、そうでないかもしれない」が私のお決まりの返

哲になった。

-intentionally-have floated into our cultural discourse:

母と義父は、とても簡単な質問にもはっきりした答えを出せない私にがく然とし、腹を立て、私は罰を受けた。しか

We really can't know if something is true or not," maxim of the deconstructionists, or Bill Clinton's infamous

い、どうやったら何にでも確信が持てるのかということをその当時の私はどうしても理解できなかったのである。私は、自分の固定した考え

quivocation, "That depends on what the meaning of 'is' is."

を含む言葉を発するよりも、自分の部屋に引きこもるのを好む

Critics of Derrida complain that if words have no essential meaning, then there is no meaning. Or, if there is, you can't actually

ようになった。デザートに食べたいもののさえ言えなかった。

communicate it. I fundamentally disagree. Design is first and foremost a language that is dependent upon

言葉が思考の第一のツールだとすると、私たちは、まず初めに言語境界を設けずに物事を認識したり、説明したりすることがで

words in order to communicate meaning. Symbols and actions

きないのだろうか。ニュアンスとは何なのだろう。曖昧さについてはどうだろうか。フランスの哲学者ジ

have as much profundity as words. In fact, facial gestures are all but universal and far more trustworthy in reading a situation than

ック・デリダは、我々は「欠点、真実も、起源もない記号の世界」に住んでいる、と述べた。デリダの哲学の中心原理の一つは「テクストと

anguage can be.

かがすべてである」である。デリダの哲学は、信奉者が言語の性質

Nevertheless, language can be helpful. Back in Tokyo, while hiring a taxi to transport me

ら意味を脱構築しようと試みているため、そのまま脱構築という名称をというにふさわしい。「実際のところ、あることが真実であるか

from the middle of Tokyo back to my hotel, I found that the elderly taxi driver had no idea what I was saying and

らかを知ることはできないという脱構築主義者の金言や、ビル・クリントン元大統領の

where I was asking him to go. As my attempts

to communicate proved fruitless, I began to ask passersby

if they could assist me. A young Japanese woman came over, and I asked her if she could help me tell

the cab driver where I

was going, as I was lost. It seemed that she understood the word "lost," and I began to

feel relieved. But before I knew it, she got into the cab alongside me and started feeling around the floor! She falteringly asked me,

"What lost?" Before I could answer, she motioned to

other passersby.

Suddenly five generous people began looking for something

I hadn't lost in and around the taxi. I couldn't help but laugh and consider the various things

one actually could lose: your confidence, your control,

悪名高い曖昧な表現「それは「S」の意
味である」などのように、脱構築の観点を表現するいくつかの語句は、意図的にあるいは意図せずに、私たちの文化的言説
に入り込んでいる。

デリダに批判的な人々は、言葉に本質的な意味がなければ、意味は存在し
ないか、あるいは、意味があっても、実際にそれを伝達することはできない、と主張する。私は、基本的にはこの考えに賛成でき
ない。デリダにとっては何よりもまず言語であり、デザインが言葉に依存しているのは意味
を伝えるためである。シンボルや行動には、言葉と同じような奥深さがあ
る。実際のところ、顔の表情はどこでも通用し、状況を読みとるのに言葉よりもはるかに信頼ができる。
それでも、言葉は役に立つ。東京の話に戻ろう。街のまんなかからホテルまでタクシーに乗ると、年配の運転手は私の言ってい
ることやや行き先を全く理解できなかった。言葉による伝達の試みが無駄だと分かって、私は通行人に手助けを
頼んだ。日本人の若い女性が歩み寄ってきたので

私は彼女に、道に迷ったので、行き先を運転手に伝えてくれないか、と尋ねた。彼女は「

your appetite, your reputation, your keys, your dog, your faith, your shirt, your heart, your mind, your life. I had

lost（失くした）」と言う言葉を理解したようで、私は救われたと思った。しかし、次の瞬間、彼女はタクシーの私の横に乗り込ん

simply lost my way. It took a few minutes, but I was finally able to correct the miscommunication

できて、床を手探りし始めた。彼女は「何を失くしたのですか」と訥々と尋ねた。

by showing the growing group around me a postcard of the hotel where I was staying, which I fortuitously remembered was in my

私が答える隙を与えず、彼女は別の通行人を手招きした。

handbag. The image

突然、5人の心優しき人々がタクシーの車内や周囲で私が失くしてもいないものを探し始

did the trick, and then all of us—the young woman, the elderly cab

めた。私は、自信、コントロール、食欲、威厳、評判、鍵、飼い犬、信念、シャツ、ハート、気持ち、命など失くしがちなもの

driver, the burgeoning crowd of helpers, and me—burst into spontaneous

をあれこれと考え、笑わずにはいられなかった。私はただ道に迷っただけなのである。数分後にやっと、滞在しているホテルの絵葉書をさら

clapping and laughing. Not a word

に増え続ける周りの人々に見せて、私は誤解を正すことができた。ハンド

was uttered, not a phrase was exchanged, but suddenly, everyone was on

バッグに入れていたのを幸いにも思い出したのである。絵葉書の写真は効果絶大だった。若い女性、年配のタクシー運転手、手助けしてくれ

exactly the same page, and everyone understood.

た人々、そして私は自然と手をたたき、大笑いした。一言もなく、言葉が交わされなか

FINAL FRONTIER

Every couple of years. I go through a period of intense insomnia, when I need to wrangle up all sorts of ways to coax myself to sleep. The most successful technique I've found thus far is to imagine that I'm soaring backward 10 billion years in time to the singularity we now call the Big Bang. Along the way, I pass unfamiliar galaxies and attempt to understand how they got there and what, if anything inhabits the odd surfaces of various planets and asteroids.

I marvel in front of a black hole and float infinitely towards the event horizon, unable to accelerate or decelerate out of the gravitational pull. Time has stopped in front of this ceaselessly gorging vortex, and I'm rendered paralyzed and mute by its power.

love

By the time I finally fall asleep, I fantasize about discovering one grand unifying theory of the universe, brashly bringing together Einstein's Theory of General Relativity and the models of quantum mechanics. This formulation, of course, is conceived by a person with no real education in science, math, or physics, and by the time I awake the next morning, I have all but forgotten the nonsensical equations memorized on my mystical journey.

Though I am severely obtuse in regard to all things scientific, it would be an understatement to say that I'm merely fascinated by the theories of our origins. However successful such hypothesizing may be as a tactic for eradicating sleeplessness, it has a vital immediacy: I wish I could bring from my dreamland space odysseys even one answer to the perplexing questions we face as a species.

Perhaps this is one of the reasons why I love science fiction and the more speculative genres of writing and entertainment. Television shows such as *Star Trek* and *The X-Files* and movies like *Star Wars* are endlessly captivating to me. So I had high hopes when I went to see the highly anticipated J.J. Abrams film *Cloverfield*, a *Blair Witch*-inspired flick (with jerky, doc-style camera movement) about a Godzilla-like alien that lands in lower Manhattan and proceeds to destroy everything in its path.

As the film unfolded, I found myself in a bewildered state, unable to believe that I had paid money to watch a film about unsuspecting civilians running through narrow city streets while barely avoiding the thundering engulfing plumes of smoke and debris from crumpled buildings. I leaned into my friend Emily and asked if she thought the movie could be a metaphor. She glumly shook her head no. "I think it's supposed to be about an actual monster," she whispered.

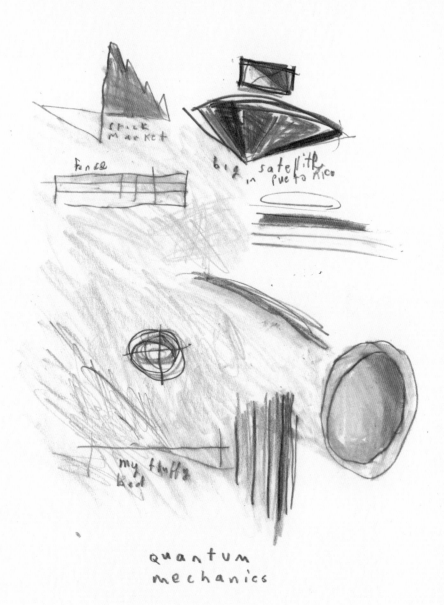

spice market

fence

big satellite in Puerto Rico

my fluffy bed

quantum mechanics

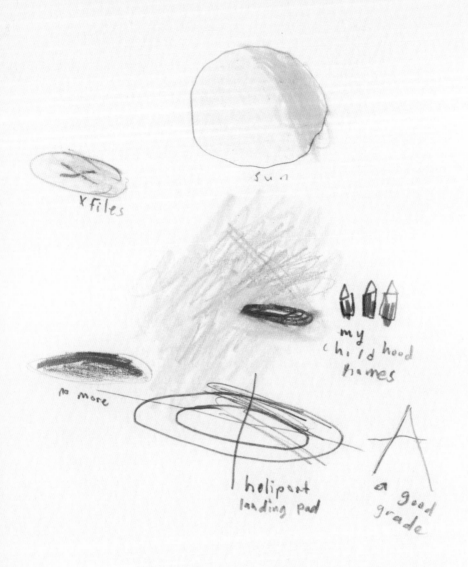

x files

sun

my child hood names

no more

helipaat landing pad

a good grade

why do we remember?

On my walk home, I passed billboards for the Will Smith movie I am Legend and for a television special on the History Channel titled Life After People. The campaigns for both the film and the program contain images of a post-apocalyptic Manhattan, and they feature familiar landscapes rendered wholly transformed by our disappearance. As I viewed the thorny, overgrown locations, I realized that somehow, in the six-plus years since 9/11, enough time had passed to now see these realistically horrific images as entertainment.

Philosophers and scientists alike believe that if humans can imagine something, there is a distinct possibility that it can be manifested. As I observed the trifecta of imagery around me, I couldn't help but wonder if we had either forgotten the horror of the past or if this horror had become so much a part of our reality that we now simply factor it into our forecast of the future. It's hard to tell.

Why do we remember what we remember? Why do we forget what we forget? In the Harold Pinter play Betrayal, two ex-lovers recall a shared experience differently, and argue about who has the more accurate recollection. Pinter makes it clear that though each character's memory is deeply felt, the validity of each recollection is highly subjective. This is both a saving grace and a hindering happenstance in our human condition.

Our memories—as frail, fierce, or fabulous as they are—help us construct our realities, our identities, and our perception of the world around us. When they fail, our world fundamentally changes, and we cease to be what we remember or recognize. Our current reality is simply a collection of overlapping memories, some shared, some not. Each memory we have is like the frame of a film that gets swept up in the sequence of images that precede and follow it. The condition of our collective memory has now become the condition of our consciousness and our culture. Our collective memory is fleeting a recreation of a scene that no one can fully remember.

One Sunday night, I once again found myself suffering from insomnia. I lay in bed, tossing and turning, reliving the experience of Cloverfield, witnessing the buildings falling in slow motion, then rewriting the film's ending and reconfiguring the storyline, over and over again in my head. And then I stopped. Why was I doing this? Why was I putting myself through this? I had no idea. And I reconsidered. Rather than relive these visions of our destruction, why not embark on my ritual into the far reaches of the universe? For though I may not have even one answer to the questions that confront our civilization, I would much rather obsess over our mysterious origins than be debilitated by our demise.

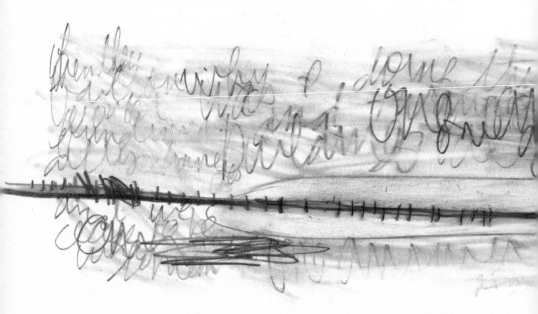

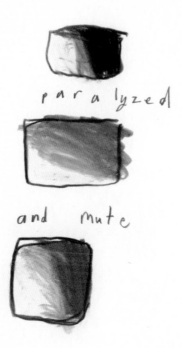

para lyzed

and mute

memory

FAIL SAFE

For most of

my life I followed a safe path. I remember in vivid detail the moment I began the journey. AUGUST 1983, the hot, MUGGY SUMMER OF "SYNCHRONICITY" AND "MODERN LOVE." A few months out of COLLEGE, I stood on the corner of seventh avenue and BLEECKER STREET IN NEW YORK City wearing pastel-blue baLLoon trousers, a hot PINK v-neck T-shirt and bright white Capezio Oxfords. I lingered at at the intersection peering deep into my future, contemplating the choice between the secure and the uncertain, between the creative and the LOGICAL,

the

known

and the

unknown.

I dreamed of being an artist and a writer, but inasmuch as I knew what I wanted, I felt compelled to consider what was "reasonable" in order to safeguard my economic future. Even though I wanted what my best friend once referred to as "the whole wide world," I thought it was prudent to compromise. I told myself it was more sensible to aspire for success that was realistically feasible; perhaps even failure-proof It never once occurred to me that I could have it all.

all

ALL

AS I LOOK back on that decision 20 years later, I try to soothe myself with this rationale: I grew up in an atmosphere of emotional and financial disarray, so my impulse as a young woman was to be tenaciously self-sufficient. As a result, I have lived within a fairly fixed set of possibilities. I am not an artist; I am a Brand Consultant. I don't work alone, painting canvases and sculpting clay in a cold and quiet studio; I work in a bustling skyscraper and create logos for fast-food restaurants and packaging for mass-market soft drinks, salty snacks, and over-the-counter pharmaceuticals.

I am not profoundly unhappy with what has transpired in the years leading up to today; most days I consider myself lucky that I have a fun, secure job and a good paycheck. But I know deep in my heart that I settled. I chose financial and creative stability over artistic freedom, and I can't help but wonder what life would be like if I had made a different decision on that balmy night back in the West Village.

I've come to a realization over the years: I am not the only person who has made this choice. I discovered these common, self imposed restrictions are rather insidious, though they start out simple enough. We begin by worrying we aren't good enough, smart enough or talented enough to get what we want, then we voluntarily live in this paralyzing mental framework, rather than confront our own role in this paralysis. Just the possibility of failing turns into a dutiful self-fulfilling prophecy. We begin to believe that these personal restrictions are, in fact, the fixed limitations of the WORLD. We go on to live our lives, all the while wondering what we can change and how we can change it, and we calculate and re-calculate when we will be ready to do the things we want to do. And we dream. If only. If only.

one

day.

SOME

DAY.

EVERY once in a while—
often when we least expect it—
we encounter someone more
courageous, someone who choose to
strive for that which (to us) seemed
unrealistically unattainable,
even elusive. And we marvel.
We swoon. we gape. often,
we are in awe. I think we
look at these people as lucky,
when in fact, luck has nothing
to do with it. It is really
all about the strength of their

imagination;
it is about how they constructed the possibilities for their
life. In short, unlike me,
they didn't determine what
was impossible before
it was even possible.
John Maeda once
explained, "The computer will
do anything within its abilities,

but it WILL do NOthing unless commanded to do so." I think people are the same — we like to operate within our abilities. But whereas the computer has a fixed code, our abilities are limited only by our perceptions. Two decades since determining my code, and after 15 years of working in the world of branding, I am now in the process of rewriting the possibilities of what comes next. I don't know exactly what I will become; it is not something I can describe scientifically or artistically. Perhaps it is a "code in progress."

The grand scheme of a life, maybe (just maybe), is not about knowing or not knowing, choosing or not choosing. Perhaps what is truly known can't be described or articulated by creativity or logic, science or art — but perhaps it can be described by the most authentic and meaningful combination of the two: poetry. As Robert Frost wrote, a poem "begins as a lump in the throat, a sense of wrong, a homesickness, a lovesickness. It is never a thought to begin with."

I recommend the following course of action for those who are just beginning their careers, or for those like me, who may be reconfiguring midway through: heed the words of Robert Frost. Start with a big, fat lump in your throat, start with a profound sense of wrong, a deep homesickness, or a crazy love sickness, and run with it. If you imagine less, less will be what you undoubtedly deserve. Do what you love, and don't stop until you get what you love. Work as hard as you can, imagine immensities, don't compromise, and don't waste time. Start now. Not 20 years from now, not two weeks from now. Now.

LOOK BOTH WAYS

I often fantasize about what
might
have been,
but isn't.

I   contemplate   what   my   life
could have been   like   if   I   had
could have been been been accepted
                           to
                      the   journalism school
I'd
applied   to
in 1985   or   the art
            program I'd   hoped
to   attend   in 1992. I
sometimes imagine what would
have
happened   if my first
a very
different
self   marriage hadn't fallen
                  apart,
                  or my second.
                        I will never
                  really know,
but I imagine that self a very
different self   with shorter hair
            and different clothes,   as if the
                  choices I made for myself
                  have defined how I look in
                  addition to how I live.

Somehow,
these other "selves"

have

                sunnier dispositions and
cleaner closets,
        and they are almost
always thinner.   They have more
money and
more free time;   they drink less,
        and they definitely don't
worry about getting older.
                        Nowadays,
they are a more secret self,
                as the memory of what

                        might have been
                        is now more of a
        projection   of what isn't than
    of what if?
        But mostly   I find myself
                        fascinated,

as I live my deeply
ritualized and entrenched life, with the idea
of this

unknown other. Who could I have

been?   Should

I have been

her?

Could I have

been her?

And what about

her?

This

        past

            summer

                I spent a lot of

time in

Albany, New York,

            the home of my alma mater, the

University at Albany,

State University of New York.

    I wasn't there to visit the school,

                            per se,

                            but rather

        rather

because my father, who lives in

upstate New York,

was undergoing

triple

bypass

surgery.

The first day

at the hospital

was

long and exaggerated,

every response analyzed, every behavior

deconstructed.

My family was fully on edge

as we waited for news,

and then when the news was   good,

we waited for physical verification.

we

But

my dad's   recovery took longer than

expected,   and three days in Albany

turned into seven.   I

spent most of my time in the hospital,

but one afternoon I headed over to the

campus that was the center of my universe so

many years ago.

Once there,

                              I retraced

          my baby steps

          in

          design

          and

          literature

          and art

          and boys and books and bands.

All

        of the offices and classrooms
still
            were locked,

      but the buildings were still

open.   I walked by

    every single structure on campus—

past the library,

through the art gallery,
        see was still
into the English Department.

I traced the embossed letters of the

nameplate   on the office

door

of my favorite literature professor,

      who I was thrilled to see was
there
still teaching.

   I ran up three flights

      of stairs in the

campus center to the offices of

the school newspaper and the

radio station and,   on tiptoes,

                    tried to peer through the

          dark windows into the

     rooms where I'd devoted

thousands of hours.

               As I lingered in the hallways,

                    I looked down at the

     surging fountain in the center of the

     campus and remembered the same view

                    in the same building

                         by the same person

                              so long ago:

               how I stood in the same spot,

     squinting in the daylight for a clue,

any clue at all,

to who I was or what I would become.

And it occurred to me,

as I stood there, that I could

simultaneously, vividly

look both ways—

backwards and forwards,

in time—at once.

I remembered longing

to know what was coming—who I would become

and how. And I suddenly saw it all over

again in front

of me. The light was exactly the same,

and as the sun fell and the summer

shadows slivered against the elegant,

lean,

concrete towers in the distance,

I recognized

the smell of the warm air,

the precise pink and grey

of the coming dusk

and the

mysterious melancholy

and joy

of both knowing

and not-knowing,

and the

continuity

that occurs

when both

collide.

When I got back

to New York City, I

went foraging through

my storage closet

looking for an old   scrapbook

that

I made in the years before   I went to

college.   The scrapbook was a

rather makeshift

affair, as I had simply   blank

used a large blank sketchbook to archive my

ephemera. This included the requisite

party and bat mitzvah invitations,

my commendations in art and home

economics, various diplomas

and newspaper clippings, and

some shredded prom corsages.

The collection also included   things

I had long forgotten

existed:

the airplane boarding pass

for a trip to Europe in 1976;

       the first cryptogram I ever solved

          from the Long Island daily newspaper,

               Newsday, in 1973;

a faded mimeographed copy of the

Lawrence Ferlinghetti poem

"The Pennycandystore Beyond the El"

with my scribbled notation

              too

      why

      does   soon

      he

      say

      too

      soon;

a handmade poster

encouraging

my fellow students to vote for me

for Senior Class Secretary of Student

Affairs in high school;

the Playbill from a 1970s evidence

production of A Chorus Line;

and most incredulously,

the original tag from my

very first pair of Levi's.

evidence

As I gingerly hugged the Playbill,

I surveyed these scraps,

this evidence of a life.

But I felt feeble recalling my desire to

document such banality.

too

soon

How foolish I was!

As I rifled through the book again,

I fell

upon the silly   little threadbare

newspaper cryptogram.   I assumed I had

saved it   because

it was the first code I ever broke,

some four decades ago.   too   But as I

re-read the content of the message,
soon

it occurred to me that perhaps

I kept the clipping because of

the quote it contained this excerpt from

Albert Schweitzer's   autobiography:

"Because I have

confidence in the power

of truth and of the spirit,

I believe in the future

of mankind."

Maybe we do collect

our scraps and our

memories as evidence

hope

of a life lived.   And

perhaps we decorate

our pages, and our

too   soon

dreams, and all

hope

of our possible

selves,

too   soon

through the

projective

too   soon

lens of what

hope

we hope for.

But maybe, as Ezra Pound so

appropriately stated,   "We do not

know the past   in

chronological   sequence.

It may be convenient

to lay it out…   on the table with dates

pasted on here and

there,

what we know

but   what we know

we know by ripples

and spirals

too

eddying out   from us   and

from   soon

our own time."